"Laura Davila is a treasure in the Mexican magic community, bringing the powerful spells and spirits of our ancestors to a whole new generation of workers. With every word, she preserves important culture and guides us deeper, as we receive the answers to ancient questions and begin to understand ourselves and those who came before in a way we never could have imagined."

—J. Allen Cross, author of *American Brujeria*

"*Mexican Magic* is a comprehensive collection of spells, rituals, and recipes that is suitable for all levels of brujos and brujas. For readers new to the craft, Davila provides both social and historical context for the modern-day practice of brujeria. She teaches us about the path of a bruja and shares a plethora of practices. The spells are practical, accessible, and easy to follow, and often incorporate everyday objects, such as food, spices, or images of saints. Davila creates the perfect recipe to help readers adapt time-honored traditions to their modern-day lives. *Mexican Magic* is a perfect book for all who seek to learn more about Mexican brujeria."

—Atava Garcia Swiecicki, author of *The Curanderx Toolkit*

"In *Mexican Magic*, Laura Davila does a phenomenal job of illuminating the creativity of Mexican culture and magic with lively stories and magical rites born out of resilience, humor, necessity, and practicality. Anyone who shares an appreciation for our culture and is interested in magic will love this book!"

—Erika Buenaflor author of *Cleansing Rites of Curanderismo* and *Veneration Rites of Curanderismo*

"Laura Davila is a fountain of wisdom, and in *Mexican Magic* she generously shares her extensive knowledge, grounded in rich histories and gorgeous detail. Her practical approach is inviting and rigorous at once. As a modern bruja and forever student of witchcraft, this is a resource I'll return to again and again."

—Lorraine Monteagut, PhD, author of *Brujas*

"Laura Davila has put in the work to preserve our culture. Her spells, anecdotes, and knowledge are gifts to our starving souls. I am impressed with what I take away from her books."

—Nix Murguia, author of the Calavera Hotel series

"Laura Davila's *Mexican Magic* invites us into the dearly kept secrets of the brujas of Mexico, leading us through the potent symbols, rich culture, and layered significance of their practice and their world. Warm, authentic, and powerful, this book is a transformative journey into a subtle and complex reality that is as practical as it is profound—where identity, faith, and power dance together to make an irrefutable magic. Laura's writing is vivid and heartfelt, and she transmits her embodied practice of the sorcerous arts, mysteries, and lived experiences of Mexican magic with skill and wisdom. Get this book—it is a treasure—lose yourself in it and gain a new way of seeing."

—Hoodoo Moses Shenassa,
founder of the Holy Mountain Spiritualist Temple

"Laura Davila's *Mexican Magic* is a profound and heartfelt journey into the rich traditions of Mexican folk magic. Her deep respect for the cultural heritage, combined with her modern perspective, makes this book a powerful guide for anyone seeking to connect with the mystical roots of Mexico. Davila's wisdom and warmth shine through every page, making complex rituals accessible and inspiring. Whether you're new to the craft or a seasoned practitioner, *Mexican Magic* is a must-read that will leave you feeling empowered and deeply connected to the magic that surrounds us."

—Christy Lendechy, bruja and owner of @BrujasBotanica

"Laura Davila writes like she is outlining the heart of magic itself, showing us how magic flows from the roots of culture, tradition, and, most importantly, lived experience. She dives straight in, effortlessly weaving practical magical concepts and crucial cultural context in a way that immediately makes the reader start thinking about how magic evolves. *Mexican Magic* also marks one of the most accessible points of entry to the Holy Souls of Purgatory for the English reader—the Anima Sola. Davila has managed to present this misunderstood class of spirits with the clarity and precision they deserve. *Mexican Magic* contains the hallmark of any good book on culture-specific magical traditions: it makes the reader reflect on how their own practice is staying alive. For those looking to walk towards an understanding of Mexican magic, this book is a necessity.

—Aaron Oberon, author of *Southern Cunning*

"In the book, *Mexican Magic: Brujeria, Spells, and Rituals for All Occasions*, Laura Davila confidently presents Mexican magic traditions with authenticity, honesty, depth, and her characteristic humor. The book stands out not just for its rich array of spells and rituals but also for its thoughtful integration of cultural context and spiritual insight. Magic in Mexico has triumphed in the face of fear and repression, evolving to thrive in the twenty-first century. Davila's inclusive approach makes complex spiritual concepts accessible to readers of all backgrounds by weaving practical guidance with the nuanced history and symbolism of Mexican magic. Davila invites readers into a dynamic and profound living tradition. For anyone interested in delving into the depths of Mexican magical traditions, Laura Davila's *Mexican Magic* is an essential guide that offers both inspiration and practical insight."

—Reverend Laura González,
priestess of the Goddess, Circle Sanctuary minister

"Laura Davila returns to expand upon her first book, *Mexican Sorcery*, and throws open the doors to her practice and the traditions of Mexican folk magic in a way not seen by English-speaking readers before. Her tour of traditional spells, workings, and spirits is incredibly thorough, offering the curious an introduction to the *animas* and the angels that have shaped folkways and beliefs for generations. Even Saint Patrick makes an appearance and demonstrates how interwoven the many cultural streams that make up Mexican heritage are! Crucially, she does not simplify or dilute these traditions—she is bare-bones honest about the nature of workings that are meant to control or even harm others, but she puts those workings in context and reminds readers that brujeria comes from a place of need and often oppression, and thus requires gravity and effort. She also clearly points out that the magic of Zacatecas is going to be different than that found in Catemaco, and no one book or person can capture the richness of brujeria completely. Still, Davila does a magnificent job here, and maintains her conversational, sometimes salty tone to fill this book with as much knowledge and enchantment as she can. You learn everything from candle spells and prayers to how to use a tortilla press in magical work, and even a spiritually charged recipe for the holiday drink *rompope* as she extends the holiday calendar to the Navidad season. This is a book not to miss if you have any interest in the magical traditions of Mexico or North America more broadly."

—Cory Hutcheson, author of *New World Witchery*

Mexican Magic

Brujeria, Spells and Rituals for All Occasions

LAURA DAVILA

daphne la hechicera, author of *Mexican Sorcery*

WEISER
BOOKS

This edition first published in 2024 by Weiser Books, an imprint of

Red Wheel/Weiser, LLC
With offices at:
65 Parker Street, Suite 7
Newburyport, MA 01950
www.redwheelweiser.com

ISBN: 978-1-57863-832-1
Library of Congress Cataloging-in-Publication Data

Names: Davila, Laura, 1984- author.
Title: Mexican magic : brujeria, spells, and rituals for all occasions / Laura Davila.
Description: Newburyport, MA : Weiser Books, 2024. | Includes bibliographical references. | Summary: "Algunos nacen con estrella y otros estrellados. This dicho (saying) roughly translates to 'Some are born with a star, while others are born starry.' It refers to the Mexican belief that good luck is a matter of fate. The same goes for magic; some people are born with a natural gift, while others look at magic as a skill to be mastered. This book offers an overview of magic from across Mexico and shares spells, magical recipes, tips, and advice on how to be a magical person and live a magical life"-- Provided by publisher.
Identifiers: LCCN 2024033161 | ISBN 9781578638321 (trade paperback) | ISBN 9781633413313 (ebook)
Subjects: LCSH: Witchcraft--Mexico. | Magic--Mexico. | BISAC: BODY, MIND & SPIRIT / Witchcraft (see also RELIGION / Wicca) | BODY, MIND & SPIRIT / Shamanism
Classification: LCC BF1584.M6 D38 2024 | DDC 133.4/30972--dc23/eng/20240819
LC record available at https://lccn.loc.gov/202403

Cover by Sky Peck Design
Interior photos by Laura Davila
Interior by Steve Amarillo / Urban Design LLC
Typeset in Bely and Baker Signet

Printed in the United States of America
IBI

10 9 8 7 6 5 4 3 2 1

Anima Sola by Teresa Irene Barrera Figueroa

Dedicated with love to all the brujas by trade, to those who inspire us and taught us that magic is everywhere, to the anonymous trade witches, and those who wrote books or were on television—Karen, Horacio, Tamara, Mizada, and many others who dedicated their lives to shaping and preserving Mexican magic.

¡Gracias!

CONTENTS

CONTENTS

ACKNOWLEDGMENTS

Scott Ihrig, *mi corazón es tuyo.*

Neil Gutierrez, *mi estrella favorita.*

Fui lo que tenía que ser, no lo que otros esperaban que fuera; fui lo que quería, no lo que debía. Fui lo que decidí, no lo que otros eligieron por mí.

I was who I had to be, not what others expected me to be; I was who I wanted, not who I should be. I was who I decided, not what others chose for me.

—Paola Klug, "Amaras al señor sobre todas las cosas"
from El Decálogo de las Brujas (My translation)

En el pedir está el dar, en el agradecer está el merecer.

Giving is in the asking, in the thankfulness is the deserving.

—Mexican folk proverb

PREFACE:
EL CORAZÓN

Mexican symbols, magic, and spirituality are based on Mexican identity, history, values, traditions, and, above all, our worldview as Mexicans. The heart is a symbol, a representation of love and gratitude, that is very common among us, a shape that has been adopted to a lot of milagros Mexicanos. The word "milagros" means miracles. Milagros are small metal pieces, usually made of tin. Each little miracle has a shape, such as body parts, animals, and plants, among others. The tradition of milagros goes back centuries, and they have their origin in cultures and religions that predate Catholicism or even Mexico as we know it today. Thus, at present, it is a sample of syncretism just like our magic and beliefs.

Each milagro has a design and decoration. Since they are handmade, they are very unique, so no two are alike. They are mainly used, as their name says, to offer thanks for a miracle or to ask for one. The tradition goes that if a miracle is granted, a milagro is gifted and placed close to the saint, folk saint, or virgin who granted said miracle. Milagros are also carried for protection and good luck. Even though los milagros are a tradition that started during colonial times in Mexico, for Mesoamerican people and our first ancestors, the heart as a symbolic and spiritual power was everything. The meaning of the *yolotl* (heart) was the most valuable gift that they could offer to their many deities, or, in the beautiful words of Miguel León-Portilla, the most reputable and commonly cited authority on Aztec culture and literature, they "offer it to those who had made possible, with their own sacrifice, the existence of the world and everything in it." The yolotl was considered the seat of life and part of their soul.

Today, in many Mexican towns, many people carry heart milagros or hang them in their homes as a reminder of the capability of trade and exchange that we have with the divine, as a symbol of the place where we carry our ancestral and cultural memories, and where our family's most cherished traditions abide within us. The place in which recipes were lovingly handed down to us with love, and where they remain because they were not written on paper with pen but rather engraved on our hearts through memories, where we hold fast our magic.

Milagros can be made of gold, silver, tin, lead, or wood. But the milagro you have in your hands right now happens to be made of pages of paper, filled with stories, recipes, songs, and magic, just like a milagro Mexicano. Use it as a reminder of the capacity of trade you have with the divine; a charm; to petition saints for guidance, help, or protection, or as an offering; or a way to reach out to a friend in times of need by sharing this little miracle with others.

Before you go through the pages of this miracle, there is something you need to know: this book is intended to be close to your heart. *Mexican Magic* is a miracle born of a unique vision. Through these pages, you'll experience Mexican magic that honors Mexican heritage, a blend of traditions that we inherited from all our ancestors from all the different and distinct regions of Mexico. There are many books on the shelves about Mexican magic and witchcraft, books that provide us with magical methods and formulas. This book is different from those that currently exist on the market because this book proposes the use of ancient Mexican magical methods and teachings adapted to today's Mexican witches. This is the book that I believe is needed out there in the world, to fill a hole in the hearts of many people, people who have a full-time job, possibly office hours, who are a parent, who have a busy life, but at the same time want to practice Mexican witchcraft in a traditional way, attached to the old ways, using appropriate and traditional terminologies, products, and ingredients.

The intention within these pages is that Mexican magic doesn't get lost, that it reaches the next generations, even in this hectic lifestyle that we lead on this side of the border. Mexican magic is the "possibility of possibilities," and its closest reach is within the pages of this book. The style of this practical, convenient, comprehensive, and heartfelt guidebook is inspired by how we, as Mexicans, learned to do magic, and how magic became accessible to the Mexican masses in the '80s and '90s. Take into consideration that the object of this book is not simply to finish it but rather to make it *yours*. Let this book inculcate and infuse itself into your own heart and become part of your magical arsenal.

INTRODUCTION:
LA ESTRELLA

Algunos nacen con estrella y otros estrellados.

This *dicho* (saying) roughly translates to "Some are born with a star, while others are born starry." It refers to the Mexican belief that good luck is a matter of fate, something we were either born with or not. Most Mexicans attribute their good or bad luck to a greater force, to God's will, even to the placements of the stars in the sky. Being born with a star is a blessing and being born shattered is a misfortune for some.

Yes, I do believe in destiny. I do believe in fate, like most Mexicans, but also like most Mexicans I believe even more in faith, virtue, and purpose. Just like there are many who are born to do magic, there are many others where life itself and being born starry pushed towards magic. Being a Mexican *bruja* is being part of a fight between what the stars say up there and what my heart dictates down below, although my faith leads me to think that the stars and my heart are linked to the plan of life that a greater force has for me.

The best *brujos* and magical people that I've had the honor to know were people who were not born with good luck, those whose destiny didn't give them a good hand of cards to play. Some others were very lucky and were born with the best cards to start the game but folded due to their stupid life decisions. A lot of these folks were not born into a family that believed in magic or even superstitions (or at least not openly). Neither did they have elders to teach them. In some cases, they didn't even have access to the internet. The only thing that they had was the conviction to become the best brujos they could be. It was not a choice, since they had no other option because their well-being and sometimes even their lives or one of their family members depended on it. They had, above all, a death or life motivation, and they soon realized that good luck is a skill to be mastered. Their necessity led them to action and their actions gained them dexterity. They were willing to go all in and risk the last thing that they had to bet with hopes of a better future: *their faith.*

The '80s and the '90s were not an easy time in Mexico. I know you may say, "Has there ever been such a thing over there?" Probably not, but this time period came with the end and the beginning of many things. My mom and my *tías'* generation was driven by the quest to provide for their kids a better future than they had, so they could be independent from their husbands and not have to endure what their own mothers and grandmothers had to endure out of necessity, while at the same time trying to abolish the traditional gender roles that our culture imposed on them since centuries ago. But they certainly had to deal with other situations that no one prepared them to handle. A lot of them moved out of rural areas to live in the big cities and to have access to other things. These women were pioneers of entrepreneurial endeavors, a lot of them starting their own businesses. They did not want a boss, a man telling them what to do. They were willing to take risks in order to succeed.

I am not sure they thought about their happiness as much they thought about their goals, but I can say for sure this time was the beginning of a cultural revolution, not only for women but for brujas in Mexico. My early teenager years were spent between a *hierbería* my Aunt Diana owned, a store that she had the vision to divide in two. In one side there was a botanica store where she also did tarot readings, and in the other half a *revistería* (a newsstand) that served as a bookstore, magazine shop, and lottery as well. Thanks to that and the fact that I was such an incessantly chattering kid, I made friends with some of those women in the store, and they began to tell me their stories.

To be honest, I don't know if I was the one who was looking for those stories, or if those stories were looking for me, because sometimes, somehow, those stories need to be heard by you. As a bruja, you grow to realize that occult forces are always preparing us and positioning us for divine appointments. Think of this book as one of those appointments between these magical people and you.

I want to start with the fact that people in Mexico see magic and witchcraft very differently from people here in the US. Here in the US, there are a lot of misconceptions spread thanks to social media. Some of those misconceptions are founded in ignorance, others in speculation, others by disconnection, and some others with the aim of profiting from these practices, somehow trying to keep them as a monopoly by selling them as a closed practice that requires initiations, baptisms, or being chosen by another person. Do not get me wrong, I support information, classes, mentorships, courses, and anything that teaches you something. I respect other people's paths and how they choose to walk them, but I want to make sure that you understand this: there are a lot of ways to get to the place you want to be.

Brujos, brujas and magical people in Mexico are not a monolith by any means. We are the sum of many factors, lifestyles, and idiosyncrasies. Our sociotechnical heritages are extremely varied: Catemaco witches are different from La Petaca witches, and even though La Biznaga witches are only 131 miles away from La Petaca ones and share a lot of the same ecosystem, they are still very different between each other. The witches of Jesús María de Los Azules in Aguascalientes are very distinct and different from all of the above. To put all Mexican witches in the same costal is wrong and contributes to erasure. Diversity and representation matters, even among small groups.

Mexico is a very large country in both cultural wealth and territorial extension. Currently, and especially on the US side of the US-Mexico border, magic is all about the titles, when in Mexico we have traditionally been more concerned with just *being,* without putting labels on what we are. There are a lot of people in our magical community who feel alienated or are greatly afraid to share and exchange magical goods that come from experiences, stories, recipes, spells, products, tips, and hacks, out of fear of being called out, just because they lacked the financial ability to pay for these mentorships or trips to Mexico. Perhaps they are afraid because they were not born into a family of brujas but, most of all, because they do not fit with the current narrative of what some authors say a Mexican witch "should" be, when Mexican witches are all walking complexities, quite different from each other. I don't think we (meaning Mexicans/Mexican-Americans) can afford to lose those experiences. Our magic and our brujeria needs people sharing those experiences to subsist! To keep feeding, to survive!

I'm not an elder. (Come on! I'm barely forty years old!) Most people considered to be elders in Mexico are sixty-plus years old. What I do consider myself to be, first and foremost, is a tradesman, an advocate, a guide, and a perfect example of how magic and faith can improve your life, your situation, your finances, your health, your luck, and change your fate. You may be wondering, what is a woman who doesn't present as an elder doing, writing book on this subject? Well, that's part of my advocacy. That's what advocates do. We write, we voice, we march, we share for our cause. Brujeria and Mexican magic, for me, is a mission. It's a mission that made me understand that the things I'm most thankful and proud to have in my life wouldn't be part of it without magic, because although I took the applause and the recognition, it really corresponded to many people who shared their magic with me in times of need: saints, folk saints, and spiritual allies. I will always show my gratitude to them and will be their biggest advocate, doing everything that I can to share their faith and their stories in the best way that I can.

I can assure you that if this book has found its way into your hands, you are supposed to read it, as well as to share its message with others. The pages of this book will reveal to you the stories, the advice, the recipes, and the knowledge of many magical people with whom I had the blessing to interact with, as well as those I observed closely as we crossed paths. A lot of them were not aware of their magical and mystical power, although some others were. There are a lot of differences among these people, in their backgrounds and their access to things. Some of them lived in the city, others in rural towns. Some were professionals with degrees, and others didn't even know how to read or write. It is all of their generosity that successfully led me along the way.

CHAPTER ONE

MEXICAN MAGIC

Depending on the culture, the word "magic" means different things in different places. Mexico is not the exception. The most accurate way to describe magic is that magic is power: the power to handle, control and exploit energy and faith in order to change, remove, or transmute something for a specific purpose according to our needs.

Contrary to what some people believe, magic in Mexico doesn't look the same today as it looked six hundred, four hundred, or two hundred years ago. Mexican magic spans across times and spaces that change every day. Magic in the Mexican sense is always adaptable. Mexican magic is imperishable because it has been a constant since the very first Mexicans were born, and that magic is reborn again each time a new brujo is born. It reproduces each time this same brujo shares their magic with others, and it reproduces again and again with *those* brujos who then share it. Think of that magic as a seed. Like ourselves, there is no way to preserve a lineage if it does not reproduce, and, in each reproduction, it mutates in a certain way to adapt and preserve itself.

Mexican magic continues to be alive and everlasting because it is not static; it is flexible. Mexican magic was kept alive when a collective embraced it, recovered it, reproduced it, adapted it to the circumstances to which it *had* to be adapted at that time to continue subsisting and for that magic to reach us. That doesn't take away the traditional component. There are certain elements that will always remain, because those components are strong. Magic in Mexico will always be powerful tool, but as with any tool throughout time, its design has developed to suit its users' needs. Consequently, every time, period, and decade has shaped our magic in a very distinctive manner.

Our magic was different during pre-Hispanic times. It changed quickly during colonial development and acquired new elements during the Mexican Revolution. I know for a fact that there are many people today claiming that their magic goes back to pre-Hispanic times. Their point is to say *their* magic is pure and undiluted. I want to be clear that the practices that I'm presenting to you in this book have strong pre-Hispanic roots, but I make no such pure, undiluted, unbroken line claims. Sadly, today Mexican magic in the United States is presented and handed down, reduced to academies, materials, and methods, taking away the principal component that allowed this type of magic to subsist: *the spontaneity*. I do consider it necessary to start linking Mexican magic to everyday life again, to our lifestyle, to our kitchens, without putting it out as a product to swallow, where "I am what I consume" statements are dominant and my magic is only as powerful as the crystals I buy, the schools and teachers I pay for, and the magical goods I can order online. That's not Mexican magic. If there is something that characterizes Mexicans and our way of doing magic, it is definitely our creativity, thanks largely to our culture. The Mexican's ability to do magic relies on practicality and accessibility.

Brujas de México

Today in Mexico there are many types of witches. There are witches who do magic and those who do witchcraft, those who are witches by profession, and the others who witch as a trade. I often use the example of things that are rustic or simple, but also as sacred as food or the art of cooking. We can all cook, but clearly not all of us are professional chefs, the kind that attended culinary school, appear on television, or cook for celebrity personalities. But that doesn't mean that we *cannot* cook at all, or, in a lot of cases, cook even better than these impeccably dressed master chefs. Experience, the desire to cook, the emotion with which we do it, and above all what our *abuelas* called *la sazón* and *la buena mano* are determining factors.

For this reason, I have come to the conclusion that doing things right is a gift, and the complexity of this is that the gift is an inexplicable "divine touch" that you will not find in a school, nor in recipes, nor in the best cookbooks, nor in the most sophisticated and carefully selected ingredients. That "divine touch," which many professional chefs lack (and perhaps do not understand), is found in many kitchens and *fondas* (dinner and breakfasts places) with women dressed in flowery and colorful aprons kneading dough. That is what makes the difference.

So are witches in Mexico born or made? Surely, they are both. Often their gift lies dormant until it *must* be woken up. Despite popular myth, brujas in Mexico are not just born: they learn, they master, they become. You may be unaware of just how much of a brujo or bruja you already are. You may be part of a large group of people that I call "the unconfirmed." Every day I receive messages from these brujos and brujas: the brujos who are *already* brujos, with a lot of experience and outstanding achievements in magic, who are waiting for someone else's validation, permission, their *confirmation*, some of them even applause. When Mexican magic and brujeria is all about agency and volition, why are you giving away your agency to others? A brujo is a being with the ability to do magic or brujeria successfully, and "agency" denotes the exercise or manifestation of this ability. Requiring outside confirmation, outside validation, permission, and even applause, takes away that agency. Agency is power; you can take control of your practice. Yes, you must take full and absolute responsibility for your own agency.

Another myth that I see constantly is that to do magic you have to have a title (like brujo, *hechicero, curandero,* or *ensalmero*), or that that title should be bestowed upon or granted to you by someone else. Do you really need your neighbors, the people who live in your county, or a stranger over the internet who you haven't even shaken hands with to grant you this agency to do magic? Mexican magic is volition, not communal imposition. Magic is a choice, a choice that no one can make for us. I *choose* to lead a magical life, I *choose* to make my way with magic, I *choose* to put my faith in my magic. Do not get me wrong, yes, there is a greater force at work. Call it life itself, choosing a few of us for this work, but that goes above and beyond human design. But it is totally up to you to put your life into service, and not the cronyism that some want you to keep believing in.

A Mexican witch is someone who opens doors and roads, who transforms problems into solutions, questions to answers, goals to achievements, dreams into realities, weakness into strength. They adapt, redefine, interpret, improvise, innovate, and take risks. They have a teachable spirit, and that's why they can find a teacher and a lesson everywhere, in every time. Every single moment is a teachable moment for them because they came to this world with an open heart and mind.

Most likely you have heard the phrase "when the student is ready, the teacher appears," but have you thought that that teacher that you have been waiting for may not appear in the way you thought? Magical guidance comes in many ways, shapes, and forms, like a song, an image, or in the folktales that many Mexicans grew up hearing. A lot of these folktales date back to long before the Spanish language or the written word. A book, a deep conversation with an *estranger* in the chance of a lucky encounter, in nature—keep an open mind but mostly a teachable spirit. What I'm trying to tell you is that you may be using the terms teachers, elders, and guidance very rigidly, when serendipity and ancestral gnosis have always played an important factor in the way we learn and execute Mexican magic.

I have to confess that I personally, even having been born and having lived almost all my life in Mexico, sometimes fell into this trap of capitalism and empty consumerism that has nothing to do with our Mexican magic. If you follow me on my social media or read my previous book, *Mexican Sorcery: A Practical Guide to Brujeria de Rancho,* you know I come from a long line of brujos in Mexico, and that magic was not always the choice I made for myself for various reasons. Even being born into a family of witches, I relate to trade witches. There are a lot of things that every trade bruja has in common, but there is certainly one that is very recurrent, not only in Mexico but in every culture, and that is *struggle.* To quote the author Julio Caro Baroja: "Witchcraft increases in moments of anguish, of catastrophes; when human existences are not only dominated by individual passions, but also by collective miseries." I agree because I have experienced it myself.

One of the greatest times in terms of contributions to Mexican magic, not only in my opinion but from my experience, was certainly the nineteenth decade, during my teenage years in Mexico. Many of you likely were not even born yet, or were little, but I can assure you that time deeply marked Mexican magic and how we practice it today.

Ando Bruja: Being Bruja

Something that I would like you to meditate on: it is no coincidence that most dictionaries containing *mexicanismos* (colloquialisms or slang) recognize the meaning of the colloquial phrase *andar bruja,* meaning being without money, without luck, or to be in need. In Mexico, the word "bruja" is more than a noun, it is a verb and an adjective, a way of being, a reaction to adversity, a consequence of adverse circumstances. Given this truism, when the propensity for magical beliefs and practices increases in Mexico, it has always been during times when the greatest economic recessions, crises, and social insecurity in our history have occurred. Regarding translations, it does not help you that a lot of things that are important to take into consideration about these practices frequently bias translations and hide important historical and cultural facts. This in turn affects people's understanding of what magic and brujeria in Mexico is and what it is about.

Every trade bruja has their own life situations that end up more of being like a calling, an awakening moment, or a point of no return, the beginning of their brujeria journey. It would be impossible to mention them all.

The '90s were an extremely difficult decade. Mexico entered a long period of economic recession. When President Ernesto Zedillo took office on December 1, 1994, he received the exchange rate at 3.41 pesos and a few days later the price of the dollar shot up to six pesos. In 1997, the dollar was already trading at 9.90 pesos, and it remained that way until Vicente Fox took power. Immediately afterwards, interest rates rose sharply, and those who had debt in dollars were hit harder. A lot of people lost their state, their jobs, and changed their *modus vivendi,* while many others took other roads unimaginable in their previous circumstances, the roads of magic and witchcraft. Moments of hardship come to shape our lives, regardless of if we are ready for them or we are not. Those moments are the best teachers. They show you the gift within yourself that you have not yet explored, that season in our lives when we are paralyzed by uncertainty but at the same time mobility becomes a life and death motivation. Once those moments arrive, we do not think too much. We act, we throw ourselves into work, into action, because we know that there is no time for doubt and perplexity. Those moments become the beginning of something new.

The best Mexican witches that I know became brujas as a reactive behavior, as an instinct of self-preservation, just because they were committed to it when they felt their lives teetering on the edge of a great abyss where they had no option but to jump. They were angry, they were hungry, they were hurt, they were tired, they were finally over it! These witches had an enormous influence on my practice and in my magic. Most importantly, they were instructing me without me even knowing. Those stories, recipes, advice, and teachings stuck with me. I applied those lessons in times of need and critical moments in the years that followed when I needed them the most. Magic and witchcraft in Mexico in the '90s were profoundly transformed. Its bases were expanded, its structure strengthened. The occult and the popular merged and the objectives became more precise; but the most relevant change, which gives the '90s a new stamp compared to other decades, was how it revolutionized an entire generation.

I emigrated back in 2010. That was my awakening moment, my point of no return, and the moment that I chose magic. We were living in collective misery in Mexico. We were in war, a war where cartels were mutilating, decapitating, torturing, and killing each other and anyone who was in the wrong place at the wrong time, including woman or kids, ostensibly over money and the drug smuggling routes that provide it. Mexico suffered one of its worst crises in 2010 due to violence, insecurity, and organized crime. For a lot of young people, their moment of crisis was the COVID-19 pandemic or even the current day, due to the significant decline in economic activity three years after COVID.

There are few things in this magical world of which I'm certain, and in the past forty years the list has become smaller. But one of the things that I'm totally convinced of is that *necessity* is the catalyst, the teacher, the school that fosters this magical foundation. Necessity is what wakes the seeker, the witch, our inner alchemist. Necessity is the ancient elder who drives us right to the root of our struggles to gain knowledge. This teacher has quite a dark sense of humor, but it is strategic and isn't afraid of teaching what needs to be taught, when it needs to be taught. Necessity doesn't ask us for permission, doesn't ask things like, "do you want to go through this lesson? Or are you ready for the next?" Necessity is the bridge that connects us to magic, but, as a bridge, *we* are the ones who must cross to the other side.

Another topic I see often that brings a lot of confusion is the gift or, as we call it in Mexico, *el don*. El don is a very complex and quite controversial topic among Mexicans, even for the ones who have lived all their lives in Mexico, so imagine how controversial it can be in the United States. A lot of people are unaware of this "don" (gift) with which they were born, the gift to become magic makers, witches, healers, to modify their circumstances, until necessity has shown it to them.

A lot of people have a misconception about what a don is and how it works. Who has it? I'm often asked things like, "How do I know I have it? What if I don't? Is the don enough to do magic? Do I still need to study or learn?" And their most important question is, how far can this "don" lead their way to their success in magic?

First, what is don? The word "don" is derived from the Latin *donum* and is defined as the extraordinary or special ability to do something. It is an innate quality, this gift we were all born with without exception, as part of our potential treasures from the very moment of our birth. But to get the work done you need more than this gift; you need purpose and virtue.

Don versus *Virtue*

Virtue is defined as action, according to Aristotle. Virtue is acting according to our gift. Have you noticed that a lot of folk prayers dedicated to saints, folk saints, and even plants in Mexico give more importance to their virtue, rather than the gift attributed to them? Virtue is the habit of being proactive, it is the impetus that our divine creator placed on us, that capacity of reaction that we must develop ourselves. Some philosophers define virtue as wisdom and ability in action. No amount of gift can compensate for a lack of virtue. (Although we were all innately born with this don, not all of us were born with the same amount, just like not everyone grows to the same height, and so some people need to foster that gift more than others.) We do not get virtue in books, in theory, in seminaries, through teachers; we get virtue through work in real life situations where our magic is practiced and tested for real. Your gift can only go as far as your virtue.

Purpose and Courage

The "gift" and virtue alone do not make a bruja; purpose and courage are also needed. If there is no purpose, there is no magic. A purpose will always create the means. The best brujas always have a purpose; the mediocre ones don't. Since there is nothing they are aiming for, there is not a driving force in their practice. Develop the ability to act on your purpose to become a virtuoso.

Courage is the virtue that allows you to face necessity, look it in the eyes, and say you are not taking from me, I'm taking from you without fear, without hopelessness, without victimhood. Magia Mexicana involves optimism, hope, and being in the right spirit. Mexican brujas know that they have the power to choose, to turn the tide and change the direction of events, that we can redirect our circumstances, our luck, and our lives. Fear is our principal enemy. Fear slows our magical progress. The best brujas walk on faith, never playing safe but without taking foolish risks either. No matter how much info you gather, how much you study, how long you walk following others, Mexican magic requires action. Fear is crippling.

Yes, when you act, you may fail, but if you never act, you will never progress. If you fail once or twice, keep on acting until you succeed. The spells that didn't work in the past, the ones I was not able to manifest into reality, are like seeds that didn't sprout. There is still part of them fertilizing the soil where today my blessings grow. A Mexican bruja does not let anything go to waste, doesn't get discouraged, and certainly does not look for confirmation in the wrong places (and by this, I mean your own biased evaluations, or those of other people). The only source of real confirmation about how effective your magic is, is time and the results of your practice. Courage must be the foundation of your journey.

A Brief History of the Don

Since pre-Hispanic times in the place that we know today as Mexico, there were sorcerers, witches, and magicians of all kinds, from those who controlled the weather, to those who could heal someone, to those who could cause harm and even death. *Forty Classes of Magicians in the Nahuatl World* by Alfredo López Austin shows us a list of various beings with supernatural abilities, although it clarifies that said list does not express the totality of all the existing abilities. This list details these magicians: through its translation it makes known how the ways in which they acted, and the ways they acquired these "gifts" likewise makes a difference between those who were beneficial and those who were only dedicated to carrying out curses.

During pre-Hispanic times, among different pre-Hispanic cultures, there were different ways to spot people with the don even before their birth. Some families knew someone with the gift was coming because, during pregnancy, the baby had the ability to get out of the womb and come back at least four times (it could even sing, talk, or have intense and prolonged hiccups). In those cases, the expectant women kept "menstruating." Of course, today we know that bleeding during pregnancy does not indicate that a baby is getting in and out of the womb, even though those beliefs still exist among some parts of the Mexican population.

Among the Aztecs, supernatural abilities were acquired on the day of birth, but there were ways to defeat or escape that destiny. Some families evaded this gift for their newborn through ceremonies. These ceremonies exchanged the magical effects of the day of birth. In other cases, congenital deformity was another sign of being born with a supernatural gift.

Lopez Austin also emphasizes that the gift came from learning. Most of these writings mention entire villages of sorcerers, and the fact that some of them were founded by someone with vast magical knowledge, as is the case of Malinalxochitl, founder of Malinalco, and other important places known for their magic.

Lilian Scheffler, in her book, *Magia y Brujeria en México*, suggests the following:

> [A]ccording to the popular conception, both those who do magic and practice witchcraft have special powers, which could be granted in different ways, like being selected by some divinity, through a revelation in which they are given powers, or acquired through learning, although the learning is pointed out as indispensable even for those with innate powers and those who acquired them from a revelation.

Today, we believe that the ability to do magic is an innate gift of every Mexican, no exceptions, or at least that is what the literary trend on magic, witchcraft and occultism in the '80s and '90s made us believe, but always with the premise that such gift must be accepted, cultivated, and developed to be paired with virtue and purpose. Otherwise it is not a benefit to have it.

As you can see, the don and the beliefs around it vary vastly in different places of Mexico and through the ages. There are hundreds of writings on this specific topic and I, myself, had the opportunity to read a lot of these writings. I made sure to quote and reference some of the most important ones in this section, so you understand that these beliefs are deeply rooted and nurtured in specific areas, and quite often one area of Mexico's beliefs contradicts other areas' beliefs. These beliefs are true for some people and untrue for some others. The assumption that there is one universal truth on topics like the gift, the path, or the way of learning in Mexican magical terms have permeated through social media to the point of alarm, due to the devaluation and loss of different cultural treasures and traditions. Mexican magic and witchcraft, as well as its practitioners, teachers, and the beliefs surrounding them are not a monolith. This book specifically focuses on *las brujas de oficio*, the identity of these witches: what these witches believe in; how they practice; and their goals, tools, and motivations.

CHAPTER TWO

BRUJAS DE OFICIO

Trade witches (brujas de oficio) are revolutionary in the spiritual warfare sense. They are brave, resilient, adaptable, and very strong. These brujas remind me a lot of *adelitas*, who were iconic women with a lot of cultural and historic importance in Mexico. Adelitas joined the Mexican Revolution in 1910, playing various significant roles that they were not even prepared for, like doctors, nurses, soldiers, cooks, logistics, and burying the dead. There was no other option but stepping up. The term "adelita" is entirely anonymous; they were just simple women trying hard, who performed the best they could under extremely arduous circumstances. Just like the adelitas, trade witches living through difficult times had to be as strong and wily as survivalists. Their character has always carried more weight than their title. Though the adelitas fought valiantly during the Mexican Revolution, they received very little recognition for their hard work during those turbulent times, just like most brujas de oficio.

The trade witch doesn't become a bruja de oficio as a result of theological or doctrine training, PhDs, initiations, or baptisms. Often their skills lie dormant until a crisis occurs in their lives or their communities, and no one better suited willingly steps forward to occupy the chair. Even though their skills were the result of hidden or casual training, which was what made this person fit for the job (trade), they have an umbrella of people that they have chosen to support with their magical knowledge. This can be family, friends, or community. Brujas de oficio needs no one handing over their power in the human sense, but her spiritual allies (the Divine Creator, saints, spirits, folk spirits, animas, Muertos, and others.) A bruja de oficio can simply choose a group to support and make themselves available to them.

Trade witches were not even called brujas or brujos. Most of the time, they were not even called by their own names, it was simple as *la senora que cura, la senora que te arregla el problema*. Meaning "the ma'm who heals," "the ma'm who fix your problems." The knowledge of the oficio witches comes from being in an arena, over a necessary period, and having gained expertise. It is hard for me to reconcile: "How do we remember these powerful women who were a pillar and the foundation for Mexican magic? And yet we also continue to alienate and underestimate the ones who became trade brujas under the same conditions or circumstances?"

Not every bruja becomes a bruja in the same way, at the same time, at a specific age, or under the same circumstances. La bruja de oficio gives other brujas a blueprint to follow in their own magical paths but without imposing, because she knows better than everyone that brujas de oficio often make their own path.

It is time for retelling. It is time for trade brujas to be known, seen, and heard.

There are a lot of trade witches in Mexico, most of them *sin pena ni gloria* ("unnoticed"). For many different reasons, most of them live in anonymity. They have other jobs and carry out other activities. Most of the time they are not full-time witches, and many do not make a business or earn profit from their witchcraft or magical products but rather perform magical services for themselves or members of their community. They are the mothers, the grandmothers, the aunts, the neighbors. They can come in any shape, in any gender, and from any background. What all of them have in common is that they are truly miracle workers; they are autodidactic, flexible. They have an enormous listening capacity and the desire to learn from everything and everyone. They are innovative, they are practical, and their faith is enough to move mountains.

Karen Lara (10/31/1958-12/23/2015) is the example of who I consider to be the most famous trade witch in Mexico and a person who was destined to become a legend and bestselling author. Karen was a journalist who interviewed personalities for magazines and newspapers. She started journaling magical recipes from other people, following them herself, and sharing them with other people in need. The story goes that when she became unemployed, by serendipity, several people in the publishing world, among them the greatest of greats, Gabriel Garcia Marquez (bestselling author of *Magical Realism* and *100 Years of Solitude*), suggested to her that she should publish said magical recipes and put out a book of magic. She got to publish most of those magical recipes during the '90s. She was a success and very well received by people who started to practice magic thanks to her recipes. The rest is history, the history of a woman who inspired a lot of people to become their own magical advocates.

I still remember many women turning on the radio to hear Karen Lara talk about magic and her infallible recipes. And that intro, with that deep voice full of hope for those who needed love, money, or protection:

> *Si la primavera trae consigo el amor, y el invierno se lleva la soledad, prepárate, y consulta, hay que escuchar a Karen Lara, quien lo mismo atrae a un amor marchito, que enfría a los amigos calurosos indeseables. Magia blanca que lo mismo requiere de un vaso de agua que de un elixir de amor.*

If spring brings with it love, and winter brings with it loneliness, prepare yourself, and consult, you must listen to Karen Lara, who also attracts a withered love, which cools undesirable hot friends. White magic that requires a glass of water as well as an elixir of love.

—Karen Lara, *The ABC of Magic.* ABC Radio (760 AM).

I wish you knew how many people became brujas in Mexico thanks to Karen Lara.

The path of a bruja de oficio is not easy. It comes with a lot of realizations, bumps, study, but most of all practice and experience. Ask yourself why you need to learn and practice magic. What are your motives to spend a lot of your time and energy on this? By asking those questions, a lot of answers are going to drop fast and become very clear for you.

Brujas de Oficio and Religión

A Mexican bruja in general is very eclectic in nature, a mixture of the ancestral and the modern, the internal and the external, the owned and the borrowed, the sacred and the profane, with little sprinkles of faith, mysticism, and creativity. We experience Catholicism as a cultural tradition, not a religious experience, because we understand that is part of it.

To go back to the cooking example, Magia Mexicana traditionally is like a *pozole*. Pozole is one of Mexico's most traditional and beloved dishes, neither a soup nor a stew but, at the same time, both. There are different regional variations, such as red, green, white, and black pozole, all of them traditional! While it is not accepted by all academics and chroniclers that the origins of pozole was as a dish for rituals and cannibalistic appetites, there is a lot of research that suggests it. Other research indicates that what was originally boiled in the pozole was not human meat, but Xoloitzcuintle, a breed of dog domesticated and bred for human consumption.

Whatever its origin, the truth is that this dish transcended and evolved over many centuries and is present in our time, just like our magic. It should even be noted that not all pozoles are prepared with cacahuazintle corn; each region of our country has different varieties of corn that have been developed based on geographic climates and the cultures of the peoples who have lived in those areas. What is true is that all pozoles traditionally contain hominy. Once you take out (or do not add hominy), it is inevitably a *caldo*. It doesn't matter if you want to call it pozole, it is still a caldo. Hominy (corn) is to a pozole what cultural beliefs are to Mexican magic.

We can't take away either the ancient components or the folk Catholicism to make it authentically Mexican. I'm referring to authenticity as legitimate and true, not uniformity or homogeneity. And what would a Mexican pozole be without oregano, lemon, chopped onion, and some aromatic herbs from Asia? Without a doubt, it would still be a pozole, but rather bland, don't you think? The same happens in Mexican magic. If we remove the components and influences, something important will be missing, Magic in general terms is as sacred and as important as eating and cooking in a culture. Mexican food, like magic, constitutes an element of cohesion on various aspects of the life of our community, our traditions, our beliefs, and the cultural and magical exchanges that are shaping identities constantly. Just as Mexican food and Dia de los Muertos (the Day of the Dead) are declared intangible heritage of humanity today, so our magic could be as well.

Whether or not you have Mexican ancestry, many people today are drawn to Mexican magic, just as they are deeply attracted to Mexican food. Personally, I consider that this appreciation of our food, our magic, our much beloved festivities and our culture in general involves a desire for knowledge and deeper understanding, and this book is an attentive invitation for all without discrimination.

La Magia para el Hogar y la Cocina: Magic for the Home and Kitchen

La cocina, the kitchen, has been an iconic part of Mexican magic for centuries. If you think about it, la cocina was our abuelas' ally, protectress, and liberator rather than the society-imposed exile that we sometimes think. The kitchen was their fortress, their hospital, their battlefield, and the place where they became alchemists. They knew well that thresholds between the physical and spiritual worlds exist within those four walls, what was hanging on them, the fire, their coffee. They knew that the power of the spirit world was palpably close. Everything was magical: the smells, the flavors, *el molcajete, el metate,* your abuela's apron.

Mexican kitchens are very magical and very distinct from other kitchens. They are colorful in every sense of the word. Every time we stop and embrace an awareness in the simple, easy, practical, and frugal ways of our Mexican magic, we honor our roots and our stories as a collective and bring with them a little of understanding and reparation, no matter how distant in time or space we think we are from those stories. These stories have had a deep cultural impact on how we feel, how we act, our worldview as Mexicans, and how we do magic.

For Mexicans, magic is born in our homes, but mostly in the kitchen. If you think about it, this makes a lot of sense. Mexicans are foodies by nature; that is why cooking and great ingredients are very present in our day-to-day lives and are part of our magic. Our kitchens are the first place where prosperity and abundance are felt and, at the same time, it is where you notice that something is not right with our economy or our finances. For us, the term "kitchen witch" really did not exist because we assume and imply that *all* Mexican witches are kitchen witches.

This book is inspired by the way magic is done in Mexico. The recipes, rituals, spells, advice, and popular wisdom are true magical gems, transmitted from generation to generation, mouth to mouth, full of knowledge and tradition. These classics transport us so we can know and be a little more familiar with Mexican culture and history, and so we can understand where the magical heritage of our people comes from. The content of this book is a direct connection with the past and will allow you to experience the essence of traditional Mexican magic in every sense. The rituals, spells, and tips are usually simple but extremely effective, and all done using basic ingredients, tools, and objects that are easily found in any Mexican home, which makes these recipes special.

CHAPTER THREE

THE ICONS

I cons are physical representations (art, statues, paintings, sculptures, and jewelry) of different spirits, both folkloric and religious. These are inextricably, associated with beliefs and often with popular superstitions.

The most famous religious icons in Mexico—which can be the images inspired by virgins, Christs, saints, and animas—have always undergone magical reappropriation by magical people. These magical people have incorporated them into their own devotion and magical repertoire. This reappropriation has given life to popular esotericism, where the occult, the folkloric, and somehow religious have all become a distinct way to experience our magic and our faith, within the reach of the average Mexican and their unique and special idiosyncrasy.

The Crucifixes and the Power of the Cross

Although the cross is considered by many to be a universal sign and a protection amulet that is used by many people in Mexico, it is more than just a decorative item. It is the perfect mix between religion, superstition, and magic. A crucifix (Latin: *crucifixus,* meaning "crucified") is an effigy or three-dimensional image of Jesus Christ crucified. The crucifix is something that cannot be missing in almost all Mexican homes or kitchens.

One of the most deeply rooted popular beliefs is in the protective virtue of a crucifix against all evil that could threaten a household and its inhabitants. This can't be just any crucifix. For the crucifix to be highly protective and highly magical, it must be stolen from the home of a couple consisting of a man named Jose and a woman named Maria. This is something that is not hard to find since Maria and Jose are the most common names in Mexico according to the National Institute of Statistics and Geography (INEGI).

La Cruz del Dia: The Cross of the Day

My parents are such hustlers. When I was a little child, my parents had several shops and still to this day my dad is a successful salesman. When I was very little they started their own business. Besides having this entrepreneurial nature, they were people of a lot of faith. Having grown up around business of all kinds, these merchants, dealers, traders, suppliers, and brokers were my first introduction to the world of money magic.

Wanting to have money, prosperity, and abundance is a human desire. It doesn't matter where we come from; all of us desire to have the means to afford a comfortable and pleasant lifestyle. There is nothing wrong with this desire; money makes our life easier. It is not that money itself is important; what is important is, after all, what money can buy, such as food, adequate housing, and education. Money complicates our situation and our day-to-day life when we lack it. We invest a lot of our time making sure we have enough money, and mental and emotional energy as well. Money and finances affect our daily living in a lot of ways.

Hacer la cruz del dia ("make the cross of the day") is a deeply rooted magical custom among Mexican merchants which consists of blessing yourself with the money received from the first sale made that day and, in this way, not only offering thanks but also multiplying your profits. The owner of the business must receive the money and thank his client from the heart; when leaving that client, he must bless himself with that bill or coins (today you can do it with the receipt copy if you use a terminal for cards). To bless oneself, a cross is made with the right hand on the upper part of the body. With an outstretched hand, the hand goes to the forehead, then to the lower chest, then to the left shoulder, then to the right shoulder. As the cross is drawn, these words are said: "In the name of the Father, the Son, and the Holy Spirit. Amen."

La Sagrada Familia: The Holy Family

The Holy Family is a Catholic icon that is venerated in many homes in Mexico. It represents all the virtues and teachings to which every Mexican family should aspire. That is simply a symbolic representation of everything we want to reign in our family nucleus: loving and protective parents, good providers, and caregivers. But what happens when the family or one of its pillars is weak due to issues such as lack of work, addictions, and infidelities? This family protection must be carried out on the third of each month as protection, and as a space and opportunity for gratitude and meditation.

The only thing you need is a place dedicated to the Holy Family in your home. You can add flowers and a representation of the Holy Family such as a painting or a statue. Every day light a white candle to the Holy Family and pronounce the following prayer:

In the name of my Almighty God, I turn to your Holy Family, to the Virgin Mary and her husband Saint Joseph, and in a special way to the child Jesus, and I invoke them in this now and in this holy moment so that they open the roads for me and for all of us who live here in this household, and are protected from any misfortune, adversity or any evil, both personally and professionally; remove, I beg you, all evil, stumbling blocks, obstacles that we may have in our walk, that for each road that passes, the steps are of peace, harmony, love, good luck, fortune, success, prosperity, work, health, tranquility, evolution, calm, serenity, that there is no enemy that walks next to me, that there is no evil, spell, black magic, incantation, witchcraft, or sorcerer that can close our paths, and if there are, that in his walk alone find the same thing that you want me.

That my ways are open and that for all of us, they appear clean, unlocked, paved with happiness and joy, and all the situations of our life as well so that we can walk through them without stumbling blocks so that we can move forward in life with fortune, good luck, success, and prosperity.

That's what it will be, through your intercession.

Amen.

La Cruz que Abrecamino: The Cross that Opens Roads

Among the countless rituals that Mexicans have developed over the years, few have as significant an importance as those associated with the cardinal points and los four rumbos, crossroads, and the Christian cross. This is what we are: a combination and syncretism of beliefs and faith. This ritual is a reminder of what was already there and what was brought.

You will need:

- One abre caminos candle or white candle

- Seven abundance grains (I like to use the following, but they can be substituted as needed: white rice, corn, black beans, lentils, chickpeas, pinto beans, fava beans, mustard seeds.)

- Four coins of the same denomination

- A big plate

- A big bowl

In a big bowl, mix the ingredients and the coins together, except for the mustard seeds. Rub the ingredients with your whole hands and put all your energy into those ingredients. Feel the rice, the corn, the beans, and all those textures for a couple of minutes. Do not focus on anything specific, this is not a spell for that. This is the kind of spell work you do where you let the Universe, God, and the saints surprise you, opening windows and doors and catapulting you out of them in ways you will have no idea were possible for you or within your reach.

After feeling the seeds and the four coins in your hands for a while, you are going to form a cross with them, and place the mustard seeds and the white candle in the middle. Light the white candle and place a coin at each cardinal point. Then say this prayer to the Divine Providence:

> *O Sweet and Tender Providence of God, in your hands I commend my paths and I entrust myself, my hopes, my fears, my desires, my callings, my opportunities, my finances. Divine Providence, open the roads.*
>
> *Amen.*

Allow the candle to be consumed and put the seeds in a pot or your garden, then throw the remains in the garbage.

Caravaca Cross

Wearing a Cross of Caravaca is one of the most powerful ways to invoke the protections of this ancient talisman. There are versions of the talisman made that are small enough for the person to carry or wear, or big enough to hang above an entry door of a business or property. The Cross of Caravaca has many uses in Mexico, but one of the most common is that it is used as an "anti-lightning" protection and is worn around the neck during thunderstorm days. It is also hung in the home. Hanging the cross on the door of a house avoids bad omens.

One of the most famous esoteric books in Mexico is La *Santa Cruz de Caravaca*, which contains many prayers for this cross. Each one is recited for a different purpose. It can also be used by combining its power with the celestial virtues of the archangels Saint Michael and Saint Gabriel in order to ask for help, as well as protection against evil entities, ill will, and envy. In Mexico, the Cross of Caravaca is also often paired with the *El Secreto de la Virtuosa Herradura*, known in English as The Secret of the Virtuous Horseshoe, which is a talisman composed from a used horseshoe wrapped with a red rayon thread and decorated with sequins and prints of San Martin Caballero.

Once you have your cross, it is recommended that you bless it and clean it with holy water (holy water on its own is enough). To clean and bless it, wet a finger on your right hand and rub it on your cross. Leave your cross in candlelight on top of a clay plate with three candles—a red, a white, and a baby blue one, representing Saint Michael, Jesus, and Saint Gabriel—before using it.

Saint George Cross to Protect
Your Home from Thieves

Household security is an issue that worries us every time we leave home, so we take measures to prevent theft, such as locks, alarms, or surveillance cameras. It is very important to protect our home from thieves, after all, and one of the easiest and most effective ways that our grandmothers had before all this technology is what I present to you with this ritual.

You will only need:

- A picture of Saint George or a prayer stamp

- A cross made of two wooden sticks and a red ribbon

- Glue

- Nails or other hanging supplies

Make a cross by tying the wooden sticks together with the red ribbon. Glue the Saint George picture or stamp to the cross. Nail or hang the cross behind the door on a Tuesday morning. When you nail it or hang it, you will repeat:

> "San Jorge bendito que se retire de mi casa todo ladron y bandido."

> Blessed Saint George, make every thief and bandit stay away from my house.

To Get Your Money Back

Did you lend money in good faith and now have problems getting it back? Does someone owe you money and there's no way to collect it? Do you give up money that someone you trusted must have paid you a long time ago?

Has your boss been telling you for a while that he is going to pay you, but you don't see it reflected in your payroll?

On a Monday, in front of an image of the Just Judge, who is an invocation of Christ, make the sign of the cross and light a candle in his name (this candle can be white or a candle of the Just Judge). Pray three Our Fathers and then say this small but effective prayer:

> *Just Judge, now that you are seated on the right hand of the Father, grant me that this prayer be listened to and fulfilled, that today I beg you with devotion, I implore you on my knees, that you go before (here say the name of the person or institution who owes you money) and with your infinite justice, make (name of the debtor) pay me everything (pronouns of the debtor) owes me, in full and without further excuses. You well know all my needs, and you know everything that happens to me, and how much I do need this money back to be able to fulfill my commitments. Grant me the payment of what is owed to me.*
>
> *Amen.*

Retorno de la Cruz Pesada: The Heavy Cross Return

A return is a *trabajo* (working) with the purpose of bringing back someone who has already left or is about to leave, even if that absence is someone who is emotionally distant. The most common returns are made for love matters, usually when the husband or wife leaves their spouse, or if the relationship is cold and lacking in passion, but there also are some *retornos* (returns) that can be done with the purpose of bringing a runaway child back home.

If your lover is wandering or they have already left, there is one simple but very effective retorno amongst our Mexican abuela's arsenal to make your beloved come back to your side, humbled, repented, and full of attention towards you.

You will need:

- A picture of the target

- A crucifix without Christ (the heavier the better)

- A stone (you can also use a paperweight)

- A pen

On a Friday, take a picture of the target and write on the back their date of birth and the nickname you call them (baby, babe, *chiquito/a*, etc.).

This return is as easy as placing the picture on a table, flat on its face and face down with a cross on top of it, and putting the stone or the paperweight on top of the cross, making this cross heavier than it is.

After you have done this, light the candle and repeat the following:

> *O my omnipotent redeemer I have recourse to the power of your cross to cause pain and anguish on my beloved, I entirely depend on your intercession so my beloved returns to me and never leaves me again (Name of the target) this cross is heavy, but heavier it will get day after day that you do not get back to me. With this cross on your back I make sure that heavy is the anguish of not knowing where I am or who I am with, heavy will be the fear of not hearing from me again, heavy will be the memories, the unfulfilled commitments, and the unrealized goals we had together, so heavy that you will not be able to carry this cross that only I have the power to remove.*

While you wait for the target to come back to you, don't call your target, do not text your target, and most importantly, do not beg. This return requires that you put yourself in a position of power, otherwise it is not going to work.

Los 1,000 Jesuses: The Thousand Jesuses

Praying the Thousand Jesuses is one of the most important magical religious traditions that exists in Mexico. It consists of invoking the name of Jesus a thousand times. In this way it is possible to defeat the forces of evil and obtain divine protection against witches and their nefarious spells and curses. To carry out this ritual, a cross is made of wood or olive branches, or we use one that we have at home. Then you will hold a rosary in your hands and repeat the following prayer:

> Holy Cross, you must be my lawyer, in life and in death you must favor me. If at the hour of my death the devil tempts me, I will say to him: Satan, Satan, you will not count on me nor will you have a part in my soul, because I said Jesus a thousand times.

All the beads of the rosary are passed, saying: "Jesus, Jesus, Jesus . . ." and so on until completing the five decades (fifty times).

At the end of each rosary, we pray:

> We adore you, O Christ, and we bless you, who, by your Holy Cross, redeemed the world. Jesus, Jesus, Jesus Christ. Oh Jesus, my Jesus forever. Jesus, Jesus in my life, Jesus, Jesus in my death. Sweet Jesus, be my Jesus and save us.

When twenty rosaries have been prayed, the thousand Jesuses are completed.

Close with this prayer:

> Oh, God, who, by remembering today the discovery of the true cross, renewed the miracles of your passion, grant us that by the value of that sacred log of life we reach effective help and help from heaven for eternal life. Through our Lord Jesus Christ, who lives and reigns with you forever and ever.
>
> Amen.

La Devocion de los Treinta y Tres Credos: Thirty-Three Creeds Devotion

Nothing reminds me more of north Zacatecas and Nuevo León's spiritual closeness than the thirty-three credos devotion. This is an old tradition that consists of praying thirty-three creeds. It has been celebrated for generations and is also known as *Devoción de las Mercedes*. Believers of this devotion use it to ask for a special favor. Thirty-three creeds are prayed in this ceremony. Each one represents a year that the Nazarene lived on Earth, and before each prayer the reason for praying is mentioned. For every eleven creeds, a favor is requested of Jesus, which adds up to three favors total. The number is in devotion to his three falls. In Zacatecas and Nuevo León, it is believed that one of the three favors that are requested with this devotion will be granted.

Mexican Scapulars

Scapulars have been a symbol of Catholic devotion for centuries and have a profound mystical meaning. These scapulars are traditionally two pieces of cloth, rectangular in shape, hanging from a string, usually with an inscription related to the virgin or saint to which the scapulars are dedicated. Since Mexico is a country with a Catholic majority, it is to be expected that many people hang these scapulars around our necks so that some saint will take care of us and protect us from all evil, and as a way of expressing devotion to a specific saint or folk saint.

Today there are scapulars sold in every esoteric store throughout Mexico and the United States, even dedicated to and with images of Santa Muerte, Jesus Malverde, Margarita Catalan, and other uncanonized folk saints who are not recognized by the Catholic Church. The scapular should be worn by the one for whom we desire the benefit or intercession by the specific virgin or saint, which means that you can certainly buy and wear the scapular yourself, or you can buy the scapular to give to a friend or family member you want to protect.

The scapulars are also a symbol of love for the Virgin Mary. It is said that the Virgin Mary promised Saint Simon Stock that those who wear the scapular would receive her help and protection and that those who died wearing it will be saved. It is believed that those who wear the scapular are protected by the Virgin Mary from sudden death, evil, ill intentions, brujeria, and all dangers.

Favorite Scapulars in Mexico

Scapular of Our Lady of Guadalupe: This scapular is used as a sign of devotion to the Virgin Mary and to remember her presence, infinite love, and maternal care as Mexicans. If you are Mexican, you are *Guadalupano* and devoted to Our Lady, even if you do not consider yourself Catholic by any means. But even if you have no Mexican ancestry, the Virgin of Guadalupe transcends cultures, languages, and countries.

Scapular of Saint Benedict: This scapular has many uses, but it is always used as protection against evil, with a great power of exorcism, to avoid falling into the seductions, traps, and temptations of the devil. It is believed to help immensely when it comes to fighting vices, like drug addiction or alcoholism. San Benito has often been invoked as a special protector and ally of mothers who need to protect their households.

Brown Scapular of Our Lady of Mount Carmel: The most powerful scapular of all. There is a belief that, for those who die wearing the Holy Scapular and go to Purgatory for their faults, the Virgin, with her intercession, will make them reach the heavenly homeland as soon as possible, or, at the latest, on the Saturday following their death. This belief is called "Saturday privilege" and guarantees whoever wears the scapular will go to Heaven on the first Saturday after their death. It is said that the brown scapular of our Lady of Mount Carmel is one of the most powerful torments against the devils.

Immaculate Heart of Mary Green Felt Scapular: Many people are familiar with the brown scapular, but not as many people know about the Green Scapular, which has quickly become known for miracles related to protection as well as healings from physical and mental illness.

Saint Jude Scapular: In recent decades, San Judas Tadeo has become one of the most revered saints in Mexico, where he is considered the patron of desperate and very difficult causes. It is believed that if, one day, you need a favor that is impossible, you should wear the scapular of Saint Jude as a way of a *manda*. A manda is a vow in Mexican folk Catholicism that is dedicated to a specific saint. The Saint Jude Scapular is considered a very protective scapular.

Scapular Use and Care

No special formula is required to bless the scapular or enroll someone in its use, although you must make sure that the wearer is using the scapular correctly. The front of the scapular should be placed on the upper part of the chest and the rear part should be placed behind the back. Never put the scapular on backwards.

Clean the scapular frequently. It is recommended to wash the scapular with fabric soap or detergent and water to keep it clean and free of impurities.

If you suspect that you are under threat of witchcraft, wash it on the seventh day of the month and the feast day of the saint to whom the scapular belongs, and leave it in a bowl with coarse kosher salt resting overnight. Afterwards, throw the salt in the trash.

The scapular is a symbol of devotion. This means that prayer, faith, and devotion are an important part of its use. When using the scapular, pray to the virgin or saint of the scapular's devotion. Keep the scapular close to you. Scapulars are a sign of commitment to your faith and worn as a garment of protection against evil and danger.

El Detente

The devotion to the Sacred Heart of Jesus has its origins in the eleventh century. "The *Detente el Sagrado Corazon de Jesus esta conmigo* (stop)"/ "The Sacred Heart of Jesus is with me," is the inscription of a shield of protection used by people in Mexico who pay special devotion to the Sacred Heart of Jesus. This is an ancient amulet that contains the image of the Sacred Heart of Jesus. It is known as a shield that God himself gives to Santa Margarita María de Alacoque so that we may be protected from the various physical and spiritual dangers that we face. It also extends a blessing of protection against the wiles of the devil for all those who carry a detente.

As a fun fact, during the COVID pandemic, detente amulets with caricatured figures of AMLO and López-Gatell, Mexican president and former Health Undersecretary, respectively, were created and sold as protection against the pandemic. Those amulets had inscriptions printed on the front saying things like "intercede" for the health of the Chief Executive, as well as a legend against his political opponents. "Stop (detente) pandemic, inflation, *prianista*, conservative, adversary, *chayotero*, neoliberalist . . . that the tiger of the good and wise people of the populus is with me."

You can use a detente in a scapular form or as a badge pinned in your clothes. It is enough to rub a little bit of holy water onto the amulet while you pray to Our Father.

CHAPTER FOUR

SAINTS OF DEVOTION

La Medalla de San Benito: Saint Benedict Medal

One of the most widespread saint medals among Mexicans, even those who practice only popular Catholicism, is the medal attributed to San Benito. This is due to its power of exorcism and in the fight against evil. The two sides of the medal have a series of letters that by themselves do not make sense. They are abbreviations for the phrases that give this item great power. On one side is the image of the saint holding a cross in his right hand and a book in his left. These medals can be placed in the home, in the car, at work, or carried on a keychain, necklace, bracelet, or any other kind of jewelry. These medallions can be found in any esoteric store or artsy shop. Its power resides largely in the faith that its wearer possesses.

Saint Antonio de Padua

Saint Anthony of Padua is known as the saint in charge of matters related to love. He was a prominent saint and Doctor of the Church. He was born in Portugal in the 12th century and his real name was Fernando de Bulloes y Taveira de Azevedo. He entered the Canons Regular of Saint Augustine at the age of fifteen, but ten years later he entered the Franciscan Friars Minor, where he changed his name to Antonio. "Padua" was added due to his stay in the Italian city in 1220. Saint Anthony of Padua is celebrated every June 13th. He is responsible according to many for uniting hearts and forming those impossible romances, as well as those that never seem to come to fruition. In Mexico, he is one of the most revered saints. Singles put their faith in him without hesitation. Saint Anthony of Padua is presented in art and statues in his Franciscan habit and with a Child Jesus in his arms, since he witnessed his appearance.

An Upside-Down Saint Anthony Statue for Marriage

Every June 13 we celebrate the Day of San Antonio de Padua, the patron known as the One of Impossible Love. Saint Anthony is one of the saints more requested by women in Mexico. Saint Anthony has helped many women find lasting love. Women, men, and people of all genders pray to him to ask for the long-awaited love of their lives. According to popular belief, in order to invoke love, a Saint Anthony statue or image should be placed upside down. Once he's upside down, tell him the following rhyme: *San Antonio milagroso consígueme un buen esposo* (Miraculous Saint Anthony, get me a good husband).

This is a very simple and yet effective ritual that can be tailored to all genders and sexualities. You only have to change the wording a little to make it suit your own needs.

This tradition is based on the supposedly true legend that San Antonio supported women in their marriages by obtaining a dowry for them. At that time, poor women whose families did not have enough money for a dowry simply couldn't get married. San Antonio, through his preaching, got many rich people to help poor women, providing them with the dowry money so they could get married.

After Saint Anthony died, a single woman visited his grave to ask for his help fulfilling her dream of marriage. As she prayed, she saw the saint on the roof of the church. His body was turned upside down. He told her to go on behalf of him, San Antonio, to a person who would give her the money for the dowry. The woman went to the place the saint had named and received the help she needed. However, when she began to tell her story to others, commenting that she had seen San Antonio "upside down," many women began to place the statue of this wonderful saint in that position to ask for help in securing a marriage.

San Pascual Baylón

San Pascual Baylón is considered the saint of Mexican kitchens. Legend has it that the friar Baylón took his steps to different convents, always asking to be a cook so he could spend more time in prayer and devotion. It is said that he had such a great faith that, when he cooked something, he always prayed, and he used to dance around the stove. That was the reason why he often neglected cooking times and ended up forgetting the dishes, and so angels came down and finished the stews for him.

During the 17th century, his image and reputation reached New Spain, and the ship in charge of transporting food between Castile and New Spain was even named after San Pascual Baylón. This miraculous saint is so tied to Mexican kitchens because we owe to him the most delicious and Mexican creation par excellence, the Mexican mole. According to the book *Mulli, el libro de los moles* by the Mexican chef and author Patricia Quintana, the creation of mole is attributed to San Pascual Baylón, the saint of cooks, when he was preparing an exquisite and rugged dish to receive the Archbishop of Puebla and Viceroy Palafox on a surprise visit to his convent.

Friar Pascual's nerves and haste were such that he tripped over a casserole where delicious turkeys were already cooked, and he spilled a tray on it that he had brought to the cupboard. That tray was full of chili peppers, chocolates, and other spices. He prayed and prayed for a culinary miracle to occur and was perplexed to see the succulent result which pleased the diners so much. This is the creation of mole.

In Mexican kitchens, it is a tradition to have a small altar dedicated to him. Even today in modern Mexico, in businesses where food is sold, you will see altarpieces with his image surrounded by ingredients and utensils symbolizing Mexicans' devotion, such as *molcajetes, metates, Talavera* dishes, chiles, and terracotta pots. He is invoked for different matters but one of the most important ones is to protect us against kitchen accidents or injuries like burning, cutting, or *enchilarse los ojos* (the act of accidentally burning our eyes with chiles by touching our face after cutting chiles).

If you need a big favor, do not hesitate to ask this saint. You must close your eyes and say:

> *San Pascual Bailón, San Pascual Bailón (decir lo que se quiere pedir) si me lo concedes, te bailo un danzón o te canto una canción.*

> San Pascual Bailón, San Pascual Bailón (say what you want to ask for) if you grant it to me, I will dance you a danzón or sing you a song.

If it is fulfilled, what was promised must be fulfilled.

To ask for a big favor from San Pascual Bailón, say the following:

San Pascual Bailón, atiza mi fogón, y concédeme buena sazón.

San Pascual Bailón, stoke my stove, and grant me good seasoning.

To Ask San Pascual to Help You Cook Heavenly Meals

If you struggle with giving flavor to your Mexican dishes, or you get distracted in the kitchen often just like San Pascual, you can ask him to help you to cook deliciously. For this you only need to repeat the following three times while you cook your meals:

San Pascual Bailón, báilame en este fogón. Tú me das la sazón, y yo te dedicó un danzón.

San Pascual Bailón, dance for me in this stove. You give me the seasoning, and I will dedicate a dance to you.

San Elias

San Elias para eliminar a tus enemigos (San Elias to eliminate your enemies).

Saint Elijah is the guardian of mankind. We ask for his protection so any harmful spirit or adversary that stalks us is eliminated (banished). San Elias helps us to obtain freedom and helps us with his power so that negative vibrations are cut and eliminated. He banishes the bad energies and all the evils sent by perverse people through magic, everything that causes us restlessness and discomfort and does not allow us to move forward.

San Elias is a great ally when doing an *abre caminos*, or road opening spell, since he will eliminate from our path any opposition that stands between us and achieving our goals. Please note and be aware that this is specifically the Mexican folklore surrounding San Elias. It is very much like the folk-lore surrounding San Alejo. San Elias and San Alejo's names rhymed with *eliminar* and *alejar* and they were emendated with those type of workings (banishment and warding, respectively). These types of workings have successfully been worked for centuries. I'm noting this because there are other cultures and countries that work with the same saints, but they have their own folklore. In other places, San Elias is known as *el Baron del Cementerio* (the Baron of the Cemetery). Do not confuse or mix things together. (Or do it, but if you do, do not say I taught you that way!)

Usually, the trabajos with San Elias involve pepper, either red, black, or in some cases both.

Saint Elijah Black Pepper Spell to Eliminate Undesirable People

You will need:

- Black pepper
- Olive oil
- Scissors
- White paper
- Black pen
- One stone collected from the street
- Black candle

Light the candle. Write the name of the person in question on the white piece of paper using the black pen. Spread the oil on the stone and add the pepper before wrapping it in white paper. Say the following prayer:

> *I, (state your name here), command, in the name of San Elias, (say the name of the target) is eliminated from my life, and you will never bother me again.*

> *Saint Elijah, I cry out to you for help to eliminate my enemy, so that he cannot hurt me, that his words do not reach my heart, that his hands cannot touch me and that his prayers have no ear, that his actions to harm me are hindered. With your help, oh mighty friend, I will be triumphant and safe from my enemy. Amen.*

When the candle has been consumed, place the stone and what is left of the candle in a place where the sun hits them, as far as possible from your house, and forget about it. San Elias knows what to do.

As you return to your home, visualize that person walking away from you and your life.

San Elias Suripanta Banishment Spell

San Elias is a great ally for any woman or man since he will eliminate any opposition. This is another aspect of this saint: helping us to achieve our love goals. One of his most valuable qualities is the way he eliminates the "*suripantas*," as my grandma used to call women who were homewreckers, gold diggers—any woman who liked a man who already belonged to another woman. This is because, according to the scriptures, it was Saint Elijah who brought judgment on Jezabel. (You can also do this spell for a *sancho*, a man who displays some of the same behaviors. Simply change the wording in the prayer to reflect your needs.)

This is a very traditional prayer to San Elias to get rid of a person who is a constant issue in your relationship. Pray it on a Friday, along with this simple ritual.

You will need:

- A sword charm on a necklace (you can purchase San Elias sword charms at *botanicas,* or find one at an arts and crafts store)

- One Saint Elijah novena candle (you can make one yourself, buy one, or use a red taper candle)

- Black pepper

- Holy Water

- A bowl

- A rag (preferably new but at least clean)

On a Friday, clean the sword necklace with holy water and the rag. Next, the sword should be placed in a bowl full of black pepper, enough to completely cover that sword. Put the bowl with the sword and the pepper very close to the candle and leave it there until the candle is consumed.

Pray this prayer three times:

> *Run, run, Saint Elijah, Saint Elijah, run, run to come to my aid, you are my Defensor and my strength.*
>
> *Run, run, Saint Elijah run. In this time of despair, give me a steadfast mind and fill me with peace as I put my trust in you, so, with Saint Michael's sword of fire, you cut all the laces, brujeria, links, lust, obsessions, and any commitments and promises made between (name of the suripanta or sancho) and (name of your lover), but above all, lend me that sword to destroy with it all the suffering, the frustration, the sadness, the insecurities, that (name of the suripanta/ sancho) has caused me, my family, (add "my kids" if you have them). I pray that I find confidence in that*

victory over (suripanta's or sancho's name) Please take control of my battle from today.

Amen.

Once the candle has been consumed, wear the necklace and pray this prayer often.

San Patricio

Mexican magic and culture have been influenced through the centuries by various cultures. One of those influences happened during the Mexican-American war. The Saint Patrick's Battalion—known in Spanish as *El Batallón de San Patricio*—was a unit of one hundred and seventy-five (accounts vary) immigrants and expatriates of Irish descent who fought as a part of the Mexican army. Most Mexicans were Catholic. The Irish, who were in their majority Catholic as well, saw the Mexican struggle against America as very similar to their countrymen's struggle against England. Mexicans started printing pamphlets persuading immigrants to desert the US army, as they felt they had a lot on common with them, much more than with the Americans.

Their banner included a bright green standard with an Irish harp, under which read *Erin go Bragh*, meaning "Ireland forever," paired with the Mexican coat of arms with the words *Libertad por la Republica Mexicana*. On the reverse side was an image of Saint Patrick and the Spanish iteration of his name, San Patricio. Today, the US Army still considers the Saint Patrick's Battalion traitors, but in Mexico they are highly appreciated, true heroes in the Mexican sense.

San Patricio's Three-Leaf Clover Amulet

In the US, the four-leaf clover has become the default symbol for Saint Patrick's Day. But Saint Patrick himself used a three-leaf clover. Saint Patrick used the shamrock in ministry, using each of the three leaves of the clover to illustrate the Holy Trinity, the Father, the Son, and the Holy Ghost.

A lot of people who use this three-leaf clover amulet consider it to be a form representing a cross. Before someone starts asking if this, in the 2020s, could be considered cultural appropriation, keep in mind that one of Ireland's great icons, Saint Patrick himself, wasn't Irish. He was brought to Ireland and held as a slave for six years. Since Mexico is a Catholic majority country, of course there is great reverence for saints like Saint Patrick, no matter their point of origin.

You will need:

- A three-leaf clover charm

- Holy water from a church dedicated to Saint Patrick

- A clean rag

- *Aceite suerte rápida* (suerte rápida oil)

- Saint Patrick candle or green candle

Place the charm inside the holy water, light the candle, and pray *La Coraza de San Patricio,* which is considered one of the most ancient Christian prayers in the world. It is called *coraza,* meaning breastplate, because it is prayed to ask for protection in the face of adversities and spiritual battles. About its origin, the legend says that the Breastplate of Saint Patrick was created by the bishop himself while he was fleeing with eight of his disciples. The legends relate that, by the work of God, they became invisible to the eyes of the druids who tried to capture them. Others say that all the druids could see was a herd of deer. This prayer was brought to Mexico by the heroic Battalion of San Patricio, and it was recited and taught to Mexicans in times of war.

I got up today. Through the strength of God that leads me: The Power of God that sustains me, the Wisdom of God that guides me, the Look of God who watches over me, the Ear of God who listens to me, the Word of God that speaks for me, the Hand of God that keeps me, the Path of God stretched out before me, the Shield of God that protects me, the Legions of God to save me from the devil's traps, of temptations, of vices, from anyone who wishes me ill, far and near, alone or in a crowd. I invoke this day all these powers between me and the wicked, against ruthless powers that oppose my body and soul, Christs shield me today. Against filters and poisons, against burns, against suffocation, against wounds, in such a way that you can receive reward in abundance.

Christ with me, Christ in front of me, Christ behind me, Christ in me, Christ at my right hand, Christ to my left, Christ at rest, Christ lifting me up. Christ in the heart of every man who thinks of me, Christ in the mouth of all who speak of me, Christ in every eye that looks at me, Christ in each ear that listens to me.

I got up today. Through mighty force, the invocation of the Trinity, by believing in the Three Persons of him, by confessing Unity, from the Creator of Creation.

Amen.

Let the charm sit in the water for three hours. Take the charm out of the water and dry it with the rag. Rub the charm with the oil using your fingers and place your charm on a necklace or a bracelet. Wash your hands with the holy water. Let the candle burn completely. Wear your necklace or bracelet.

San Mateo for Tax Problems

Like any other working person, I know that taxes are a headache. In some places, they are almost robbery and something that takes a lot from us when they must be paid. Saint Matthew, a tax collector who was turned into a soul collector by Jesus, is the person to turn to if you need an extension, discount, payment plan, or anything to do with tax matters.

The Apostle Matthew, also known as Saint Matthew, was one of the twelve disciples of Jesus. He is honored as a martyr. No one knows for sure where or how he died; several sources say that he was stoned. If you do need him, do not hesitate to do this ritual.

You will need a brown candle, and on this candle, you are going to write with a wooden toothpick the amount you owe in taxes. Then take a piece of paper with the amount you owe in taxes written on it. Place it under a plate and, if possible, use a copy of the collection paper. Wet it with holy water collected from a church dedicated to San Mateo and put it under the plate with the candle on top. Light the candle.

While you light the candle, read the following prayer:

> *Pious Saint Matthew, with your divine power and authority, make these collectors have patience with me, so I can pay everything that is owed, and if your magnificent charity reaches me, may all my tax debts get lessened or even cancelled, give me your blessings, Saint Matthew, and clear and open my work paths so I can progress, and in that way, I can comply with my legal and labor commitments.*
>
> *Amen.*

When the candle goes out, take the paper and put it under a stone or a paperweight anywhere in your house to push a fast, favorable resolution.

CHAPTER FIVE

ANGELS

I n Mexico, angels have become part of popular culture. Regardless of the Catholic religion in which the majority in this country professes belief, it can be said that many Mexicans believe that angels exist and play an important role in their lives, in their luck, in their protection, and in their finances.

Just to give you an idea of the significance of angels, one of the most emblematic symbols of Mexico is *El Angel de la Independencia* (the Independence Angel), one of the monuments most recognized and loved by Mexicans. The Angel of Independence was built in 1910 to commemorate the centenary of Mexico's independence. Its design was carried out by the architect Antonio Rivas Mercado, who conceived a masterful structure, crowned by a winged female figure holding in her right hand a laurel wreath, a symbol of victory, and in her left a broken chain with three links, representing the country's emancipation from Spanish colonial rule.

Meet Tu Ángelito de la Guarda:
Your Guardian Angel

The word angel comes from the Greek *angelos*, which means messenger. Angels in Mexican folk magic are particularly important because they bridge the gap between our physical world and the spirit world.

Angels are God's messengers and intermediaries, conveying his wishes to humankind, but they also guide, protect, and teach us. We love to work with angels and archangels in this type of magic. One of our favorites is Saint Michael the Archangel, who is adored instead of Tlaloc (which in Nahuatl means "He who makes things sprout"), the Aztec rain God. This Archangel inherited the power of fighting the bad air and bringing the rainy season. We work with the other six archangels as well, but mostly with Gabriel and Rafael.

I know it is very tempting to start working with archangels or with the saints or folk spirits first, but why would you knock at Saint Michael's door without trying to go to your own angel first? Do you know the name of your own guardian angel? Try to work with it before any other spirit.

This is a common practice taught to us as small children in Mexico. The Guardian Angel is portrayed in prayer stamps, statues, wall art, and medallions, among other art forms, as a tall angel guiding a small boy and a girl over a narrow bridge crossing a beautiful river. (It is well known in Mexican beliefs that the physical and spiritual worlds are divided by water.) The Angel de la Guarda prayer is often the first prayer children learn in Mexico, even before the traditional Lord's Prayer (*Padre Nuestro*). It is often taught to us as soon as we start speaking. This becomes a very personal and deep way to start connecting with the spirit, and a sign of protection and security. It is often recited at night before bedtime.

This Mexican folk prayer is recited as follows:

My guardian angel, my sweet companion, do not abandon me, neither by night nor day, because I would get lost. Amen.

A Guardian Angel statue.

You will need:

- Any angel image (such as a stamp, statue, pendant, or figure—the only requirement is going to be that you feel comfortable with that image.)

- Angel de la Guarda prayer.

- White candle.

- Glass of clean and fresh water.

- Any incense that you have handy.

To do this ritual and connect with your angel, you should try to be in an environment where you are free from disturbances and can feel relaxed. Even the most experienced practitioners need to be able to do magic in an area where they feel comfortable and will not be disturbed by everyday things like the phone, doorbell, or other noises. Get rid of unnecessary clutter. The area should be always tidy and clean. Having a clean space with no dust will help you breathe easier.

Take a shower, preferably during a full moon before you go to bed. Set the stamp or your image close to a window and light the candle and the incense. Sit down comfortably on your bed, inhale through your nose, and exhale through your mouth. Do this breathing exercise seven times.

Close your eyes, clear your mind, and focus on your guardian angel. The first name that comes to your mind is the name or what you are going to call your guardian angel. It does not matter if it is not a common name. Every time you need your guardian angel, it is going to be easier for you to call it by name.

After this first contact, you have access to your greatest protector.

San Miguel Archangel: Saint Michael Archangel

Saint Michael the Archangel is the leader of all angels and of the army of God. He is a warrior prince who has a main *encargo* (responsibility), which is to combat evil. The holy prayer of Michael defeating Satan is one of the most popular depictions of this archangel.

My favorite way to work with Saint Michael, and the way *mi abuelita* taught me, is with his symbols of devotion. All the angels, saints, and folk saints are known by their own symbols of devotion. But what *is* a symbol of devotion? These symbols are elements that, when we see them in artwork, statues, or other images, we know that what is actually being depicted are these spirits. These symbols are rich and full of hidden meanings and messages about devotion and faith, demonstrating why their believers trust in them. Saint Michael Archangel is often shown with a spear, sword, armor, banner, and/or scales. The most significant symbol among Mexican people is the sword.

Saint Michael's Sword

San Miguel's Sword protective amulet.

Saint Michael's sword is one of the most magical and protective amulets, and it comes with a very mystical and beautiful prayer. In this prayer, the powers of his sword are invoked to defend us in our daily battles. The only things you need are a Saint Michael Candle or a red candle (in case you can't find the Saint Michael candle). a glass of water, a Saint Michael sword charm (you can find one in any occult shop), and Saint Michael's oil. You can find Saint Michael's oil online or in any occult shop, but if you have any blessed oil that you would like to use instead, that's good as well. You will also need lots of faith.

Today would be a really good day to invoke the powers of his sword, but if you prefer to wait until the closest Tuesday that would be ideal. To consecrate your sword, just rub it with any Saint Michael the Archangel oil or any blessed oil on a Tuesday and leave it in *velacion* (close to candle light) for seven hours. You can use a red candle or a Saint Michael prayer candle. Repeat the following prayer three times while the candle is lit.

> *I, (here say your name), wield in my right hand the Sword of Power of the Archangel Saint Michael to cut off any evil force. Saint Michael's sword protects me. Saint Michael's sword opens my paths. Saint Michael's sword fights against my enemies. Saint Michael's sword is my strength. Saint Michael's sword represents me in the final judgment. Saint Michael's sword defends me in battle. This mighty Sword of Lightning Blue Light watches my back wherever I go. In the name of Adonai, the God of Israel, I declare that Saint Michael is at my right, at my left, behind me, and above my head. Amen.*

Saint Michael oversees your protection. Inwardly ask him to let you feel his strength and give this same protection and strength to others who may need it. With this symbol of devotion, you are protected by two of his qualities, which are strength and protection. Feel secure as these powerful energies now surround you.

A seven day Saint Michael's Sword candle, available at botanicas.

Saint Michael's Scales

It is very common for Archangel Michael to be portrayed holding scales; these scales often weigh the souls of people. This popular symbol of devotion is related to other saints and folk saints. In my opinion, the most important one is—yes, you are right again!—La Santa Muerte. Scales as a devotional symbol represent justice. These depictions are born from folk beliefs; the Bible doesn't mention Saint Michael weighing souls on scales, even less so Santa Muerte. However, the Bible is clear about Michael's role in helping people who have died. This is the reason behind the fact that a lot of brujas include Saint Michael in their Santa Muerte altars.

When you need justice or balance you can work with this aspect of San Miguel Archangel. Say the following prayer:

Beloved Archangel Saint Michael with the virtue and grace
that God has conferred on you, I come to you, hungry for justice.

Work in my cause against my enemy who has wronged me. I request the righteousness of your scale.

Saint Michael the Archangel, listen to my prayers, which come from the need I have and make my enemies suffer for the injustices they have committed against me.

May your divine balance calm this thirst for justice that I have at this moment. Amen.

Saint Michael's Shield

Pride is the characteristic of someone who has an exaggerated idea of themselves, which can lead to arrogance. The root of such behavior is insecurity. Dealing with people like this in our family, workplace, or school is not just a challenge but a serious headache. This shield of protection will help you to create a barrier of protection between the prideful person and yourself or someone you are training to protect from someone else's pride.

Humility cures pride by removing one's ego and boastfulness, therefore allowing the attitude of service, but if it is someone in our work place, a teacher, or anyone in a position of power in our lives, they are an ass! The best thing to do to create a humility shield is to get yourself a Saint Michael's prayer stamp or image, one where the shield is the focal point of the image and carry it every time you are going to have any kind of contact with a prideful prick.

This only works if you visualize a shield that protects you and projects humility back to the proud, somehow acting like we are giving a *cachetada con guante blanco* (literally "slapping with a white glove") which means "responding to aggression in an elegant/nonviolent manner." With this ancient but helpful magic trick, usually the prideful person shows themselves up in a ridiculous way.

Angel de la Abundancia
Angel of Abundance

Even though the Catholic Church does not recognize the existence of the Angel of Abundance as such, the statue of this angel, dressed in a green tunic with a cornucopia full of gold coins at his feet, is present on many altars and in a little corner in some shops.

Ask this angel for prosperity, abundance, and divine wealth, and to provide the necessities to attract material and spiritual wealth, as well as luck in business and any endeavor. If you need any extra help, some good advice is to invite this angel to your home or shop. You can find a representation of this angel in any botanica, esoteric, or occult shop. Next, light either a green taper candle or an Angel of Abundance candle to focus on your intention.

To invite this angel and its virtues to your place, grab the candle with both hands and concentrate as you ask for a particular abundance or fortune related situation. Ask this angel to come to your home or business to help you, using your own words. An example of this would be something like:

> Angel of Abundance, knowing of your great power I invite you to come to my home/business and grant us material blessings and the abundance and prosperity that this place needs to meet our needs. I beg you to cover this place with your sacred wings and protect it from all that brings ruin and poverty. May you bring good luck, opportunity, and good fortune to my home/shop.
>
> Today and forever, amen.

Place the Angel of Abundance on a little altar along with any items you would like to place in this sacred space. Some good ideas would be money to attract more money, clean water, sandalwood, flowers, pictures of people you need to financially support, such as your kids, or items related to your shop or business.

Cure a Common Cold with Saint Rafael

The archangel Rafael, whose name means "God has healed," is a powerful archangel and one of the favorites of Mexican people, especially among those who work in the medical field. He can assist you with any kind of pain or disease.

Curing a common cold is quite easy with Saint Rafael's intercession. You will need:

- A Saint Raphael candle or green candle

- A red or white onion

- Vick's VapoRub

- Thick socks

Instructions:

Peel an onion (white or red) and cut it into thin, flat slices. Place the onion slices on the soles of the sick person's feet after having previously massaged the feet with Vick's VapoRub. Secure the onion slices with thick, tight socks so that they remain in place. Do this right before the sick person goes to bed. You can place several slices on the arch of the foot or make a kind of platform along the entire sole. Remove the onion the next morning after letting it act overnight. Place the slices inside the stocking and leave them next to a lit candle for San Rafael Archangel. Leave it there until the candle is consumed. When the candle burns out, tie a knot in the stocking and throw it in the trash.

CHAPTER SIX

ANIMAS

Although the Catholic Church does not count these spirits, known as animas, as a main entity for Catholic devotion, there is an ingrained custom and devotion among Mexicans and other Latino groups. We inherited this custom many generations ago and we have made it our own, aside from Catholic belief, dogma, and traditions, even though it is rooted in its nature in them. This devotion makes us turn our faith and hopes to these souls that are suffering in purgatory, praying for their quick deliverance and relief, while at the same time they are also prayed to and asked for intervention in different matters such as love, lust, money, good luck, protection, and many others.

According to Catholic beliefs, purgatory is where the souls of the deceased who have not completely traveled the path of holiness lie, and those who, when dying, have not condemned themselves to go to hell. Since they sincerely repented of their mortal sins before dying, or if the faults that they committed could be cleansed through spending some time in purgatory, there were a lot of saints who held this devotion, according to popular belief. One of these saints was Catherine of Siena, who said that the souls in purgatory who have been freed from their suffering will never forget their benefactors on earth and will intercede for them before God. It is said, too, that their prayers protect their benefactors from dangers and help them overcome difficulties.

When you grow up as a witch, surrounded by other witches, you have a totally different relationship with spirits and animas than when you come to your gift later in life. The relationship is different because, when you're young, you really get to know different spirits and animas, their stories, their pain, their sins, and, most importantly, how you personally feel around them, even if you are not exactly working or praying for them. You get to feel their presence in your life, in your house. But you learn as well that some spirits *require* more attention than others, and you shouldn't be working with them unless you are one thousand percent committed to that relationship.

My grandma loved to work with las animas. She prayed constantly for them, contributed in holy and profane ways to the exaltation of purgatory and the souls detained in it who would receive relief with the prayers, but when I was a child, she forbade me to do so, or even ask the animas for any favor. As a neurodivergent and very, very young witch, who started in the craft really young, she knew I was messy and forgetful due my ADHD. I would probably forget their water and their coffee on Mondays!

To develop a relationship with the animas requires a lot of commitment because they need a lot of our prayers and our attention, even more when you are working with animas condemned for eternity like Maria Celestina, and relief is the only thing you can offer to them. After my grandma died, I was finally diagnosed and medicated, and I started developing an intimate relationship with some of her favorite animas. In this relationship I was not a spectator anymore. My personal relationship started very casually but respectfully, and it was grounded in intention. I started praying first to Maria Celestina Abdégano AKA the Anima Sola (the Lonely Soul) and asked her for her *amparo* (protection) twice a year, once during November and the other on March 8 (International Women's Day). I still pray to the Anima Sola especially hard those days for my sisters in Mexico. Women in Mexico, especially in rural towns, are being murdered, raped, and disappearing at an alarming rate. Our girls, our teens, and our transwomen are suffering femicide and gender-based violence over there every day. This was my way of being with them. Some women walk, some protest, some sing, some write, some paint. I pray, I do spirit work. That's how I contribute.

Then I started to get closer and closer in prayer and devotion to Anima Sola. This practice and devotion among brujas are sacred, but at the same time profane. This devotion in Mexico is a free and voluntary devotion that the Church approves without compelling it. I would say that, in Mexico, they don't really promote it. Since we have made it our own, the Church frowns upon our ways because they're loaded with a lot of heretical and magical aspects and components from colonial times. Praying for the souls in purgatory is an act of the love, faith, and compassion that we have for those forgotten souls—since they alone cannot purify and alleviate their sorrows for themselves—so that they can achieve eternal rest.

For this reason, dedicating a prayer to the souls in purgatory with great faith, and even offering a candle, a glass of water, and attention to them, will help them carry out their painful purification process. If you dedicate a prayer to souls on Monday, which is the most auspicious day, this will help you to begin to establish a closer relationship.

A lot of people offer novenas to these souls starting the 24th of October and finishing them on the 1st of November, but the whole month of November is propitious to ask for these souls for a favor and to offer a libation. In folk Mexican culture it is common to ask for favors from the animas. They are known for granting favors through the use of candles, glasses of water, cigarettes, prayers, black coffee, and pan dulce. (Imagine what you would offer to someone who was waiting somewhere.) Those items are placed at a certain time during nine Mondays. This prayer can be used for different purposes. Sometimes novenas are lit for love, sometimes for money favors, and other times to even get rid of enemies. The animas are very noble and usually they don't require a lot of ritualistic work, but will require a lot of devotion, attention, and faith.

You are going to see a lot of spells that involve animas in Mexican magic for all types and sorts of things, but I wanted to tell their stories specifically in this chapter, so even if you encounter these animas in other chapters, you have an introduction. Introductions, especially in spiritual and magical matters, are very significant. When you meet a spirit or anima you don't know for the first time, an introduction encourages you to start a conversation and expand your magical network. You don't have to work with all the animas. If you do work with all of them, you can still have a favorite or one you feel more confident around.

Las Animas Faith in Mexico

My favorite historical period by which to understand Mexican folk traditions is the Mexican Revolution, which was an extended sequence of armed conflicts in Mexico that took place from November 20th, 1910, to December 1st, 1920. After that followed the Cristero War, when most of the Catholic population in Mexico rebelled and fought for their religious freedom at the cost of their very lives. President Plutarco Calles launched a direct attack on the Catholic Church using articles from Mexico's Constitution, which created this counter-revolution against the Mexican government during that time. The original rebellion was set off by the persecution of Roman Catholics and a ban on their public religious practices.

Those times were hard; it really did not matter if you were rich or poor. The violence, the hunger, the fear—it was a complex time, but the Mexican revolution and the Cristero War profoundly shaped folk magic and religion. A lot of pious women became the priests of their neighborhoods, gathering in secret to express and transmit their faith, of course with a lot of "variations," I would say, from the Catholic canon.

My grandma used to tell me a lot of stories from those times. One of those stories was about La Senora Tacha, who was very close to my great grandma and who used to always keep a candle lit for the souls in purgatory. She was very punctual, and she never forgot to light that candle every Monday at 7:00 p.m. She had a special devotion to the Virgin of Carmen and Nicholas of Tolentino, who the Catholic Church considers the patron saint of souls in purgatory. This devotion was such that she had a small altar with their images and other representations of other animas. She kept this altar hidden because she was fearful in those extremely dangerous times.

The rape and murder of civilian women was commonplace. The old woman used to live with her two beautiful young daughters while her husband was fighting. A lot of those *bandidos* knew that the women were by themselves and so they were a target. One of those nights, a man who wanted to rape the youngest daughter for his twisted-minded perversions peeked through the window to see if the mother of the girls was already in bed. When he saw a large number of people inside the house instead, his surprise was such that he had no other option but to run away as fast as he could from their place. He was so shocked that he did not even make an attempt to enter or even spy on the girl again.

Intrigued, he went the next morning to offer his services to the neighbor of said woman and find out who else lived with them, but when he asked, the neighbor informed him that they lived by themselves and they never received visitors, which intrigued him even more. He told the neighbor that the previous night he had passed by very late, and he had seen people, to which the neighbor replied that he should talk to his wife since she was a good friend of the owner of that home. Later that day, he encountered the neighbor's wife, and, after telling her everything with all the details, she told him that it was because of the altar of the animas!

In every house where there is an altar with the candle to the Virgin of Carmen and Nicolas of Tolentino, it will always be protected by las animas, and all of the house's inhabitants as well.

Dominios: Dominance

This type of workings is one of the most famous and iconic in Mexican magic. I know as a fact that a lot of people who are foreign to our culture may have an erroneous idea or even feel to some extent indignation to read about this infamous practice. I want to start with the fact that this magic comes from resistance; it was born from necessity and suffering.

In 2023, dominance and passivity are gender neutral concepts. There are just as many dominant women as there are men or any other gender. But especially in Mexico due to *machista* culture, it was not always like that. In fact, we deal a lot with machismo still to this day, and I don't think it is only in our culture. It's part of Latin American history. You might think the assignation of gender roles was merely a religious matter, but no. It was a civil matter in Mexico for many years. In order to explain, you have to have a deeper understanding of what your abuela, or your tia, and even myself back in 2001 during my first marriage, were signing up for when we got married in Mexico.

I'm going to include Mexican history here, so you have an idea about the cultural context that was, and still is, engrained in the Mexican psyche and way of acting. In 1859, it was established that religious weddings had no official validity, and that, from that moment, the union of two people was a civil contract with the state. The Epistle of Melchor Ocampo is a letter that was written with the addressees to those who were getting married, since it was part of the Civil Marriage Law. This is an excerpt from Melchor Ocampo's epistle.

The woman, whose main attributes are self-denial, beauty, compassion, shrewdness, and tenderness, must give and shall always give her husband obedience, affability, attention, comfort, and advice, treating him with the reverence due to the person who supports and defends the household, and with the gentleness of one who does not want to exasperate the abrupt, irritable, and hard part of oneself.

This used to be recited as confirmation of the civil union between a man and a woman, without recognition of same-sex couples and based on harmful gender stereotypes. Many state congresses maintained the obligation to read said epistle in their codes until on February 28, 2006, when the Chamber of Deputies issued an exhortation to the different state governments that they no longer use said epistle in civil marriages in Mexico.

Men legally and culturally assumed a dominant role in Mexican society, where they were encouraged and, to a certain point, obligated "legally" to exercise control over women. Animas and spirits are the best magical allies for *desesperos, dominios,* retornos, and *endulzamientos.*

But first, what does domination mean? The word "dominate" comes from the Latin *dominare* and means "to have under one's power." Its lexical components are: *domus* (house), *-inus* (suffix indicating relative to), plus the suffix *ar* (termination used to form verbs), meaning the ability to manage, master, control, regulate, suppress, or restrain to will. Domination is done to exert power over, subdue, hold tight, and make it so that this person completely surrenders their will so we can exercise our control over them.

The most common domination work is done to control a sentimental partner in love matters, but there is also monetary/financial domination, sexual domination, and many others. The degree of domination can go from harmlessly benign with good intentions, to destructively controlling. For dominios, you can invoke the help of some animas, spirits, saints, martyrs,

An Anima Sola Shrine.

and others. To speak specifically about animas and *espiritus*, they can help you with other types of workings too, because they are very versatile. You can use candles, powders, and oils such as Dominion Oil or *Yo puedo mas que tu, yo domino a mi mujer, yo domino a mi hombre*.

El Desespero: Despair

This is a type of trabajos where the objective is that the emotions of the target overflow, to cause them to react impulsively or primitively. Their aim is to cause anxiety, anguish, and in some cases remorse and suffering in our target, due to not being with another person. The target experiences a feeling that their life has no meaning without being with the person doing the desespero, and the target loses the ability to enjoy or carry out their daily life if they are not close to the person who is working them magically. Some side effects are insomnia, loss of appetite, and a feeling of hopelessness. Desesperos induce the target to a limerence state, a state of involuntary obsession with another person. This is a different experience from either love or lust.

Prayer to the Despair Spirit

Spirit of despair, you who know and live in desperate despair, I come to you to offer you this candle and this glass of water so that you come to my aid.

So you bring (name of the person you want to despair) despair of love for me, and that despair makes (target's pronouns) to look for me.

Because (name of the target) cannot be a moment without me.

That (name of the person) dream about me, and that I be the only thought of this person when (target's pronouns) sleeps and when (target's pronouns) wakes up.

May (name of the target) gets very desperate every hour that (pronouns of your target) does not spend by my side.

Make (name of the target) be bowed down before me.

Spirit of despair, I know that you will grant me everything I have asked for, so I offer you this in gratitude.

You must repeat this prayer on five Mondays in a row and every Monday give a glass of water and a white candle as an offering.

Maria Celestina Abnegano El Anima Sola

Let us start with *La Reina de las Animas* (the Queen of Las Animas). She is known as this not only in Brujeria Mexicana but also in a lot of different traditions. Anima Sola, which literally means "lonely soul," is a highly venerated soul in Purgatory. She is usually depicted as a woman chained and standing in vivid flames. Praying to the Anima Sola is a tradition of love and devotion.

According to legend, a woman whose name was Maria Celestina Abnegano was one of the women following Jesus Christ on his way to the Calvary. She had in her hands a pitcher of refreshing water to give away to drink, and she shared this drink only with Dimas and Gestas. Out of fear, she did not offer Jesus even a sip, so she was condemned eternally to Purgatory as a punishment for her actions. The versions of her story vary from place to place. In one version, she is accused of having been a sorceress who exchanged her soul to be with the love of her life while she was alive.

The Anima Sola is one of the most famous spiritual entities in Mexico. Even today stories and legends continue to be woven around this famous figure. The truth is that she has become a part of Latin American spiritual culture and folklore.

Favored people or devotees of Maria Celestina the Anima Sola include people with urgent needs or requests, terminal patients, charities, people in long distance relationships, and people struggling with poverty or illness.

Prayer to Maria Celestina

 Maria Celestina, blessed spirit that for love and a slight to our Lord eternally purge your faults in the purgatory, I ask you to go to where my beloved is, and do not let (say the name of your target) rest, sleep, or eat until (target's pronouns) calls me and looks for me again.

By the powers of the purgatory, by the presence of fire, by the hope that fills the hearts that are waiting in purgatory to be released by our prayers, that my beloved cannot be still without me, even for a moment and that (target's pronouns) sees me, listens to, my voice, smells my perfume/cologne and always feel my presence, everywhere (target's pronouns) go.

I invoke the thirteen blessed purgatory souls to come to my aid and bring my beloved before me bowed, meek and humble.

That my beloved bathe in the essence of my desire and lust and return it to me tripled so that (target's name) never desire and feel lust for another person and that my beloved only have eyes for me and so be it, Maria Celestina, Queen of all souls in purgatory, I beg you to bring (target's name) back to Me as soon as possible, and that (target's name) feels sane only by my side, that (target's pronouns) feels that (target's pronouns) misses me and is losing (target's pronouns) mind every minute (target's pronouns) is without me, so that my beloved comes to see me and that my beloved begs me that I never abandon (target's pronouns) and make (target's name of your target) come to me with love and desire.

So be it and so it will be and so it is done.

Juan el Minero: A Special Anima Devotion in Zacatecas

The case of Juan el Minero is a well-known story of a soul in purgatory, specifically in Zacatecas, Mexico. An Inquisitorial document from the 18th century contains the story of Juan el Minero, since he was a cult that was investigated by the Inquisition. There are so many stories about this anima, but the most famous one in Mexico is that Juan el Minero was a miner working in the mines of Zacatecas who was executed by being publicly hanged. But even though he was executed, he died in repentance, and that is why he is cleansing his faults in purgatory.

Juan el Minero was well known for being a thief who dedicated himself to breaking into the churches and cemeteries to rob and vandalize whatever he could. It is said to that he was a drunk who used to go to cantinas after work and that he had an encounter with El Charro Negro. Juan el Minero really enjoyed stealing sacred goods, such as candles, and sometimes he looked for the holy waters and discarded them just for attention. For this disrespect before these sacred places, he had to suffer the spiritual consequences of his acts. One of his most obscure and outrageous sins was that he tried to rape and kill a nun.

Juan el Minero was very profane in his acts. That's why a lot of devotees don't consider him as an evil man, but rather a mentally instable one, and that's the reason why he is called Juan el Loco (Juan the Crazy) by some devotes as well. Since immemorable times, we have prayed to Juan el Minero for love and money matters.

Juan el Minero's favored people include charcoal burners, miners, gold diggers, people looking or digging for things like money, riches, fame, answers, or love.

Prayer to Juan el Minero para el Amor, la Buena Suerte y el Dinero

Anima of John the Miner, to which everyone prays to ask for love, good luck, and money. Today I came to you with a lot of faith and devotion to ask for help so that through your prompt interces-sion I find a quick solution to my problems, that my overwhelming needs disappear, that I always have a reciprocated love, a well-paid job, and good luck in all my plans and projects. Don't let things go wrong, help me to see the light at the end of the tunnel! I promise to share my devotion to you with those most in need and to spread your miracles, so that no unfortunate person will ever suffer such pressing needs as the ones I now have. Amen.

Juan el Perdido's Fame in Mexico City

One of the most traditional retornos amorosos performed in Mexico is called *El Retorno del alma de Juan el Perdido* (the Return of the Soul of the Lost Juan). It is said that any person who is not in a happy relationship or who has been abandoned and who wishes to bring their significant other back to their side, docile, unconditional, and loving again, should say this prayer that was found in the bedroom of Cleopatra, Queen of Egypt. With this prayer she was able to bring back to her side as many men as she wanted, including the famous Marco Antonio (Mark Antony).

This prayer is usually printed and distributed close to churches and markets in Mexico City. There are several steps that often vary depending on the location and person selling this secret.

Juan Perdido's favored people include single ladies, ladies looking for marriage, pilgrims, wanderers, and travelers.

Prayer to Juan el Perdido

> *Soul of Juan lost, soul of the four winds, I ask you with all*
> *the faith in my heart, with all the strength of my guts, I ask you*
> *to forbid another person to steal love and affection of (name of the*
> *person who you want to return to love you) and that you bring my*
> *lover back to me humiliated, surrendered, kneeling at my feet, as*
> *soon as you can.*

After you say this prayer, light a purple candle and focus intensely on the person you want to return to your side. After you do this, repeat the following passage.

> *Soul of Juan, the one like my beloved is lost. Return my*
> *beloved, make (beloved's pronouns) feel lonely and lost without my*
> *presence. Listen to my prayer, Juan el Perdido.*

Pray this prayer for nine consecutive days, starting on a Friday.

Anima de la Anacahuita from Nuevo León

In a town called Icamole, in the state of Nuevo León, after the Mexican Revolution, there was a small chapel about five kilometers from the town. (Icamole is about twenty kilometers from the center of the city of García.) This chapel was the place of the confrontation between the Villistas and Carrancistas. As expected, there were many deaths due to the war. Among them was a soldier named Roberto Cisneros Jaramillo, who was abandoned by the survivors of the battalion. Two days later, two goatherders found him and, seeing that he had suffered from great agony, they decided to bury him at the foot of an anacahuita tree.

They only covered his grave with stones to prevent the mountain animals from eating his body. The shepherds, afraid that they would not be believed by the soldiers, did not tell anyone what they had done. Days later, people began to say that they had seen a soldier sitting in the *anacahuita*. (the anacahuita tree) This is how the legend of the soldier's tomb began.

Years later, a railroad worker stopped near the grave at dawn to ask the soldier's soul to cure him of his high fever. In exchange for curing him, he would take charge of giving him a decent burial. Once the driver was cured, he kept his word.

After all the time that has passed, many people from different places in Nuevo León, and from the entire nation, come to this chapel to ask for something from the soul of the soldier. Some locals say they still see the spirit of the soldier roaming around that place. All kinds of favors are asked of this famous soul. You can ask him for a favor just by praying three Our Fathers for his soul and lighting a small white candle with the prayer that, one day, he will be able to rest.

Favored people include soldiers, military, people looking for any kind of help.

Anima of the Metropolitan Cathedral of Guadalajara

This soul, so famous in the state of Guadalajara, is the soul of a friar who pays for the suffering of numerous souls that he freed from purgatory by mistake by giving them absolution at the end of the mass.

Favored people include beggars, cheaters, doormen, and people who needs absolution or forgiveness.

Las Animas de la Basura y Magia en la Cocina: Trash Can Animas and Kitchen Magic

I know when many people read "trash can animas," they will wonder, *and what does the garbage can have to do with kitchen magic?* Well, believe it or not, the trash can is a portal that allowed our grandmothers to communicate with the souls they called *las animas de la basura* (the trash can souls). These souls help you find your lost objects.

To request their help, simply talk to them. All you must do is go to your kitchen trash can, light a *cabito de vela* (a tiny candle) for them, and just ask them to help you to find what was lost. It doesn't have to be a material possession. There was a time in my life where my faith was lost, and I asked las animas de la basura to help me find it back. One of my aunts lost her kid at a fair and she called me desperately crying. I immediately lit a tea candle next to my kitchen trash can. I asked the animas to help me find my niece and I prayed three Hail Marys for their release in payment and thanks for their prompt help, and, in exchange for it, they efficiently helped. My niece was back to my aunt the same night.

Anima del Retiro: Anima of Retirement to Get Rid of Undesirable People

Anima del Retiro is known as the soul of retirement, one of the many souls who are waiting in purgatory, purging for her sins. This anima is represented by the Ace of Swords card in our folklore.

The Ace of Swords in the *Baraja Espanola* deck is the symbol of power, of destruction, of defeating the opposition that we find along the way. It represents the strength, the vigor, the directness, and the will to destroy everything that pretends to defeat us. It is the righteous sword that has the difficult mission of separating the true from the false, bringing justice and truth.

I usually make my own Anima del Retiro candle, since it is not really a popular candle at the botanicas I visit often. This candle will help you make undesirable people get the hell away from you and your home.

You will need:

- A writing utensil such as a pen or marker

- Ruler

- Printer and/or decorating materials such as markers or paint

- Scissors

- Glue stick

- A plain prayer/devotional candle

- A sheet of plain paper

- An image of the Ace of Swords

- A glass of water

This is very easy. Take your Ace of Swords image and cut it out with your scissors. Glue the image to the candle glass. You can decorate your candle more if you desire.

Write the following prayer on your paper and cut it out so it fits on the back of the candle. Affix it to the back of the candle.

> *Holy soul of retirement, I call you and invoke you so that with the power that you have, remove my bad neighbor, all my enemies, and those who pretend to harm me; take them far away from my sight, this place, and any road that crosses my path.*
>
> *This candle I light for you, amen.*

If you have a picture of your neighbor, *suegra* (mother-in-law), *cunada* (sister-in-law), or anyone you want to stay away from you, put it under the candle. While it is unlikely that a candle with a paper wrapper will catch fire, it's always best to be careful. Anima del Retiro is very volatile and very protective. Never leave this or any other burning candle unattended and check it periodically to make sure it's burning properly. While it is burning, keep a glass of water next to the candle. When the candle burns completely, you can use that water to sweep your entrance.

We usually work this on a Saturday or a Monday.

Las Trece Animas Benditas del Purgatorio: The Thirteen Blessed Purgatory Souls

The Thirteen Blessed Souls of Purgatory are a group of souls who, according to folklore and popular tradition, always walk together because they work as a team to solve the most difficult issues. They consider themselves as intercessors before God because they have already achieved certain concessions by being blessed. The power to grant what is asked of them with great faith and devotion, as well as protection in difficult situations and urgent matters, is attributed to them.

In the Catholic belief, it is said that these souls are those faithful deceased who have been freed from purgatory and have achieved divine grace, although in Mexican folklore it is said instead that these souls, despite having paid their sentence and having been redeemed, are still in purgatory due to the great love and appreciation they feel for Maria Celestina, the Anima Sola.

The Adopted Favorite Spirits: Aphrodite

Thanks to the fact that Mexico's history has been marked by an enormous number of cultural clashes and exchanges, magical Mexico is full of diversity even in its magical icons. There are magical icons that have been adopted from other places and cultures and have become part of the Mexican magical repertoire, even given a very important place in botanicas, hierberia and many *mercados* shops, as well as in the homes of many Mexicans who trust in the magic of these beloved magical icons.

One of the most requested and available talismans after the Tetragrammaton in any botanica Mexicana is the Aphrodite (Afrodite) talisman, in any of its forms or modalities, for intimate and romantic attraction. Aphrodite is an ancient Greek goddess of love and beauty, identified with Venus by the Romans. She is primarily known as a goddess of love, beauty, sensuality, eroticism, and fertility. According to some sources, she presides over marriage.

In Mexican talismans, Aphrodite is portrayed with long hair, seductive eyes, and pale skin, in a posture that invites erotic imagination. Her medallion regularly has the word "Venus" inscribed, as well as the phrase *Afrodita la Diosa del amor* (Aphrodite the Goddess of Love). Love talismans, in the Mexican sense, date back the creation of time, way before Mexico was a state. It could be said that since humanity itself began to place its destiny in multiple divinities, they translated and carved them into different materials, especially metals and wood. These divinities, which have different domains of intervention, have not only crossed lines of time and space, but also cultural divides. These divinities have specific attributes and characteristics that will help you increase the strength of your love magic.

Sensual love is a magical, captivating, and exciting energy, and just what we want to attract into our lives through the virtues of this powerful and mythical talisman.

For the consecration of this talisman, it is important to carefully choose the date and time that this ritual will be performed. It is advisable to do it on a Friday, specifically in the hours that correspond to Venus. These can be found online.

Light a piece of charcoal and place it in a censer. When the charcoal is incandescent and no longer sparking, add the following mixture:

- One tablespoon of dry red rose petals

- One tablespoon of dry damiana

- One tablespoon of catnip

You can use a small spoon to pour the mixture onto the charcoal. Immediately after adding this mixture, it will begin to burn and give off a scented smoke. Pass the talisman (already hanging from a chain) through the smoke seven times, concentrating on your desire intensely. In this way you are amplifying the power of Aphrodite in your own life. Direct that emotion into your hands and then to the talisman and repeat:

> *Aphrodite, I summon your powers, to grant me these favors for which my heart longs.*

Your talisman has been consecrated. Wrap it, preferably in a red silk handkerchief, with a piece of copper, the metal ruled by Venus.

CHAPTER SEVEN

MAGICAL MEXICAN INGREDIENTS

Oil in Mexican Magic

Oil is an indispensable product in Mexican cuisine, since it has nutritional, ritual, medicinal, and cosmetic functions. Magical properties are attributed to many oils, and oils are substances associated with magical virtues and correspondences. Today we rely not only on cooking and plant-based oils for our magical purposes, but those from botanica stores as well.

Abre Caminos: To Open Your Paths

My grandmother used to say that, for all terrain people, those people who are four-by-four, there are plenty of roads. These people can make an opportunity out of every problem. But all the magic recipes and powerful spells are useless if we refuse to open our minds and dare to leave our house.

Sometimes the roads are already open, only our minds are closed to change, to the different and the unknown.

When you find yourself in complicated situations or a crisis, when you feel that the roads are closed and you are stuck, draw a crossroads on your left hand and rub some abre camino oil on your hands. Once it starts to get warm, even hot, rub the same abre camino oil on your temples and get ready to amplify your options, to become a four-by-four person. And yes! That implies a certain discomfort sometimes, such as moving to another city or country, getting another job, quitting certain habits, being able to see the big picture, and having faith.

Oil and Water Ritual to Separate a Couple

Disengagement magical tactics can be used in every Mexican kitchen with two simple but effective ingredients: oil and water. This ritual is going to help you separate a couple. It's very simple. This powerful ritual will make one of the targets (the water) disapprove of the other, making them icy, distant, and creating smugness. Meanwhile, the other target (the oil) will withdraw from any meaningful interaction with the other in very avoidant ways.

You will need:

- Two pieces of brown paper

- Oil

- Water

- Three small glass containers with lids

Write on each piece of paper the full name of each person in the couple that you want to separate. Place water in one of the containers and oil in the other. Submerge one piece of paper in each container; one in the water and one in the oil. When each container has the targets submerged in it, leave them to marinate for seven days. After seven days, pour the water from the container where you let the first name marinate and the oil where you let the other name marinate into the third container. Repeating the following sentence:

> Like water and oil that repel each other, that do not integrate and hate each other, so I want the same to happen with (names of the people to be separated), so that they can never be united, nor at peace with each other.

Close the bottle and shake it vigorously every Friday night.

Pinole Magic

We are often so quick to get out of challenging situations that we fail to grow through them. If you usually have a goal of getting out of teachable moments through your spell work, you are not getting anything out of your spell work or learning anything from that situation. We tend to be so focused on the spirit changing our situations that we act rapidly, and, instead of ten or twenty years of experience, we gain a year of experience repeated ten or twenty times. We want to spell work away every challenge, and some of those challenges are actually a great opportunity to grow up, an opportunity to learn. The ancestors knew that not every situation needs to be banished but simply worked through. Sometimes we need only to ask for strength and endurance for a particular situation.

I'm going to share one of my grandma's favorite ingredients for those exact moments when endurance, energy, and strength are what you need. This ingredient is *el pinole*. Pinole, also called *pinol* or *pinolillo*, is roasted ground maize, which is then mixed with a combination of cocoa, agave, cinnamon, chia seeds, vanilla, and other spices. Pinole has historically been used as a source of fuel for endurance and is considered an energy food. It is easily made at home, but you can buy it at Walmart as well. My grandma used to dress candles with pinole, and she also used it in spell work when endurance, energy, and strength were required. A lot of brujas from my *rancho* still use this for love because it has a lot of cinnamon, brown sugar, and honey in it, and of course it can be used for sexual spell work.

Tortillas and Related Magic

Tortillas are one of the most important elements of Mexican gastronomy and are used in a wide variety of typical Mexican dishes. Tortillas have been a staple in Mexican cuisine for thousands of years. They are rich in cultural heritage and are steeped in stories from around the table, occupying a unique place in the hearts of Mexicans. If there is something that cannot be missing in our kitchen, in our magic, superstitions, and on our table, it is tortillas and the instruments and ingredients necessary to make them and keep them warm and soft.

Cal Cross

An ingredient that some would consider controversial is cal, or calcium hydroxide. Calcium hydroxide is an odorless white powder. Mexicans have been using cal to process corn for a long time. They soak raw kernels in water mixed with calcium hydroxide. This makes it easier to process corn into flour.

In Mexico, a deep-rooted tradition at funerals is the lime cross, which is placed where the deceased is held. It is more common for this ritual to be carried out in ranchos, where funerals take place in homes.

In los ranchos, it is still customary that, when a person dies, their body is laid on the ground with their head on a manta and their body on top of a cal cross (lime cross), which represents the three hours of agony that Jesus Christ spent on the cross before dying. When laying the deceased on top of the cal cross, it represents that they died in the same way that Jesus died.

To place the lime cross, a ritual must be carried out. For the ritual, the community must place five candles on the cal cross; one each at the head, arms, feet, and one on the left side. A glass of water is placed on the right side of the deceased body. The lime cross must remain in the same place for the nine days that the rosaries last for the deceased person.

A Tortillera to Oppress and Reverse Positions

One of the most important machines that remains in use in Mexico to this day is the manual tortilla machine. It is without a doubt an ally and friend of all our grandmothers for the work and annoyances this machine saved them. Although most of our grandmothers loved to make tortillas, a little help in the kitchen is always good. Even if you are not related to Mexican culture, and even if you don't have a tortillera in your own kitchen, you might have seen one of them in a Mexican supermarket or maybe in an old-fashioned Mexican restaurant.

A tortillera is round. It can be made of metal or wood, and it is used to forcefully flatten any ball of corn dough to create perfectly round tortillas (when the ability to strategically create these balls is taught by a more experienced cook). Making a perfect tortilla is an art and a skill that we acquire with time and practice.

This Mexican artifact, so practical and so useful in our kitchens, is also an indispensable magical ally when it comes to dominating and putting pressure on something or someone. This machine has the magical power to dominate, subjugate, and oppress another person. To oppress means to keep our target down by unjust, usually heavy force, an authority holding our target down, putting them down by force with all our strength.

With this press, we are eliminating the target's freedom of action, since this person will feel a lot of weight on their head (mentally), on their shoulders (physically), and their soul (spiritually), making them feel a heaviness that will prevent them from acting normally. Our grandmothers used this artifact to deal with situations of abuse or contempt. There are numerous cases in which tyrannical partners made life unbearable. For our grandmothers who faced these tyrannical partners, this artifact reversed the situation in their favor, or what they called *darle la vuelta a la tortilla* (turn the tortilla). This saying colloquially in English would be something like "turn the tables," which means to change the situation in the other direction.

With the help of this type of artifact, we can get our target to give up their command and thus obey our orders, in addition to feeling dominated with an incurable heaviness of body and spirit. A small revenge that, in many cases, serves as a motivating lesson.

If you want to dominate something (such as a difficult situation) or someone, or if you find yourself in a weaker or more vulnerable position in relation to someone else and you want to change to a stronger position, you will need:

- A tortillero in good condition (metal tortilleros are encouraged over the wooden ones)

- A picture of your target (if you do not have one, write their name and date of birth on a piece of paper instead)

- A black sachet

- A black candle

- Optional: If you have masa or maseca and you like to craft your own poppets, the masa de maize poppets are the best to use for this kind of working. This is if you are more of an experienced bruja.

On a Monday night, gather everything you need for this trabajo and place the target's representation (either the photo or the paper with their name and date or birth) inside of the black sachet. (If you cannot find a black sachet of the right size, use a black plastic bag! Do not complicate things for yourself!) After, place the sachet in the middle inside of the tortillero. Light the black candle and repeat the following in a commanding and very heavy tone.

By the powers of the dominating spirits, today I crush you and
keep you oppressed, (target's name). By the heavy power of my will,
I oppress you (target's name) and I make you bow before my feet.
May you submit to my commands. May your life be controlled,
shaped, and kneaded by my hands while your will become as mal-
leable as dough and your desire be appeased by this heaviness.
From now on, it will only be me who dictates your actions. May this
tortillera keep you under control.

Close the tortillera and leave it close to candlelight until the candle has been consumed completely. Once it is consumed, keep the sachet or the black plastic bag with the representation of your target inside hidden and away from your target.

A Tortillero to Warm Up a Cooling Relationship

This is best to do at a waxing moon on a Friday, when the person you love is far from you, if your relationship is going through a bad time, or if there are constant fights between you and your love. If your relationship has cooled off, you better get a *tortillero* for this love ritual. A tortillero is a tortilla holder and cover made of different materials such as wood, palm leaves, or other plant materials, and its purpose is to store and insulate tortillas.

A tortillera is a tortilla holder and cover made of different materials such as wood, palm leaves, or other plant materials, and its purpose is to store and insulate tortillas along with a cloth napkin placed inside to wrap and hold the tortillas. A tortillero helps them stay soft after they have been heated. For this spell, you will need:

- A picture of the couple together
- A tortillero with lid
- A red cloth napkin
- Six warmed up tortillas

Grab the tortillero and place the red cloth napkin inside the tortillero. Place three tortillas inside (the hotter the better) and then add the picture facing down. Cover up the photo with the other three heated tortillas and then wrap everything up with the red napkin. Cover with the tortillero lid and repeat the following:

May the heat of my love and my desire for passion bring back the heart and lust of my beloved.

Now touch your tortillero with your dominant hand and say the name of your beloved three times.

Once the tortillas are cool, grab the picture of you and your lover and place it under your partner's side of the bed, wrapped in the same red cloth. Keep using the same tortillero for its original intended purpose, which is to keep your tortillas warm.

Traditional Plants

Aloe vera and cactus are both succulent plants that thrive in Mexico. They are popular for their medicinal, protective, esthetical, and practical uses. However, these two traditional plants belong to two distinct families. Cacti belong to the family Cactaceae, while aloe belongs to the family Asphodelaceae.

El Nopal

Within Mexican gastronomy, the *nopal* is one of the most traditional foods. The nopal (prickly pear cactus) is part of the Mexican cuisine and identity. Thus, it is observed everywhere: in the emblem of the national flag, in daily life, and from the kitchen to beautiful works of art, such as painting, sculpture, embroidery, and even beautiful famous phrases and poetry. The nopal is an important source of healing and magical resources.

Magically speaking, where I am going to focus, its thorns, its flowers, its fruits, and its slimy interior all have a magical quality and virtue, which make this succulent and popular cactus one of the magical ingredients in the Mexican kitchens of the past and the present.

A Nopalera to Protect Your Home or Business

Placing a cactus outside of your house will serve as a barrier against bad energy or ill intent that surrounds the premises. When growing a *nopalera* for your home, choose a pot with generous drainage holes at the bottom (you can pot it yourself as well).

To Torment and Cause Irreversible Harm

Get two *pencas* of nopal (prickly pear cactus pads). The greener and spikier the thorns, the better. When you return home, take a doll or a photograph of the victim you aim to torment, and put it between the pencas. Place them in a clay pot or on a Mexican clay plate. Afterwards, pour the melted wax from a black candle over the pencas and the representation of your victim. Once this is done, repeat the following.

> *I invoke all the spirits of sadness, pain, and regret so that you suffer and dwell in agony. (Here say the name of the person), may you pay for the affliction you caused on me. By the thorns and thistles, your will and pride be trampled on by me, may your sovereignty be humiliated while the rugged path of life brings you an unhappy future, may all the spirits of torment be your eternal companions for the rest of your life and afterlife, you will not rest for a second and may the spirits of torment not let you live in peace or comfort ever again.*
>
> *So be it.*

Prickly Pear to Protect Your Love from Any Love Spell

The *nōchtli*, or prickly pear in Nahuatl, is one of the most symbolic fruits of Mexico. It has many nutritional and magical properties, and it is delicious. The ancient Aztecs used it to heal wounds. Likewise, it prevents cardiovascular diseases since it contains an alkaloid called *Cantina*, which helps reduce heart problems, and it is said to protect love in couples.

The nopal produces a fruit called *tuna*. The tuna symbolizes the human heart. If you are in a courtship or marriage, Mexican tunas are an excellent ally so that no one can separate you and your partner through spells or *amarres*, so you can stay together and keep loving each other. With this ritual, just let anyone try to break what you and your significant other have built with a lot of commitment and affection: your relationship. May your love not be defeated by envy or by those who want to see your relationship broken and suffering for personal and egotistical gain.

Tuna skin can range in color from green to purplish red. The ones you need are the red ones. The little spots you see on them are not thorns, but they are covered in glochids, which are like little hair-like splinters that can stick into your skin and are very painful and very hard to see. When picking a prickly pear cactus fruit, you must protect your hands. They have most likely been scrubbed to remove the tiny splinters when you find them at the local market, so you may need to ask the produce people to sell them to you in their raw form (with the splinters). The splinters are essential for this protection ritual. Unfortunately, the fruits available at markets are not worth purchasing as they do not ripen well once picked and you need the sweetest tuna for this ritual.

Once you have the best magenta/red tuna, I recommend wearing gloves when prepping this protection or by using kitchen tongs. Start by cutting off one end of the fruit. Remove part of the pulp so you can introduce your filling. Fill the tuna with a spoonful of corn syrup and small pieces of nails and hair that belong to the couple in question. For better results, drops of the couple's blood may be added. Wrap the tuna in a red cloth and bury it near a nopalera (prickly pear patch) on a Friday night.

La Sábila: Aloe Vera For New Business Owners

Don Armando used to say to us all the time: *muchachos* profits are better than wages. He used to be a man of a lot of faith and really good ideas. Just like Don Armando, many of us have dreamed of starting a new business. Some have dared, and others have failed in the attempt. It is not easy to start a project where we invest all our capital but, without a doubt, something that has helped many new Mexican entrepreneurs is their faith and a little magic. One of the things I remember the most about Don Armando's shops is their *sábilas* (aloe veras).

Aloe vera is a traditional plant, used not only for display in Mexican homes. It is extremely common to see them at the entrance of businesses, shops, and stores, since this plant is easy to care for and it has been said that it drives away negative things such as envy, gossip, jealousy, and witchcraft, as it also attracts prosperity, abundance, and money. However, to make the most of its virtues we must take care of it, and carry out the following steps:

- Choose aloe vera that looks healthy, that attracts you to it, and that its size fits the space where you want to place it.

- Choose a clay pot. Make sure it has good drainage and fill it halfway with soil.

- Place three coins on top of the soil in the shape of a triangle. When you place the first coin, repeat: *In the name of the Father.* When you place the second, repeat: *In the name of the Son.* And when you place the third, say: *In the name of the Holy Spirit.*

- Place the aloe plant in the center of the triangle created with the coins.

- Cover the coins and the aloe with the remaining soil.

- Take a red ribbon and tie it with a small image of Saint Martin of Tours of the highest possible quality, making a red bow with the image.

- Water the aloe with holy water and repeat the following prayer:

> *Virtuous Aloe Vera, bless this business with your virtues and your power. Fill its owner with wisdom, patience, and creativity, that everything that is sold in this place is to the liking and benefit of its customers so that they return and recommend us to their friends and relatives.*
>
> *San Martin Caballero, I place my trust in you, so that you can combat envy, selfishness, and the evil intentions of my jealous competitors.*
>
> *That the Lord Jesus Christ, his Father, and the Holy Spirit allow this place to be full of prosperity and abundance, and that just as Jesus multiplied the fish and loaves of bread and fed all his people, make the production and profits multiply in this business for all of us who depend on it.*
>
> *Amen.*

To care for your aloe vera, avoid keeping the plant in direct sunlight all day. This is a plant that can tolerate the sun, but you should never give it more than four continuous hours of exposure. You can place it in an area where the sun hits it in the morning for a while. In this way the leaves will not suffer damage from the sun's rays. It will be enough to water it three times a week, depending on the intensity of the sun and how hot it is on those days. The only thing you must make sure of is that the soil remains moist.

If you follow the aloe vera care instructions and your aloe still gets sick, weak, or dies, it is time to perform deep cleansings before preparing another aloe, since this is a huge sign of witchcraft or a lot of envy against your business.

El Pápalo Méxicano to Make a Wish Come True

Pápalo (pronounced *pah*-pa-low) is an herb that has grown in Mexico for centuries. In several Mesoamerican cultures, pápalo was consumed as an accompaniment to food. Today it is still used to season many foods in traditional Mexican cuisine.

The word "pápalo" comes from the Nahuatl language word *Papaloquillitl*, which means "Plant with butterfly wings." *Pápalotl* means butterfly, and *quilitl* means quelite, or edible grass. The scientific name is *Porophyllum ruderale*.

Butterflies, for our first ancestors, were a symbol of rebirth and transformation. In our history, the Mexicas called them *quetzalpapálotl* and associated them with the goddess of beauty and flowers, known as Xochiquétzal. According to popular Mexican folk beliefs that are based on our history and many of our legends, when you want to wish for happiness, blessings, and you want to make a wish or request come true, you must only whisper your request to a butterfly and release it. In return, grateful, the butterfly will fly with your request and what you requested will come to you. It makes a lot of sense, since the energy of the butterfly is always with us during transformational and transitional times.

If you need to ask for a specific blessing in your life, or you need a wish to come true, you need only to take a seat in your kitchen, write clearly what you are asking for, and place the paper with your petition between two pápalo leaves. Tie them with a tiny orange cord and "release" (leave it) it in a place full of nature.

Flowers and Fruits of Love

The meaning, the language, and the symbolism of flowers and fruits in Mexican magic has its roots in so many places. These meanings existed even before Mexico became a state, starting with Xōchipilli and Xochiquetzal, who are both Aztec deities associated with flowers, sex, pleasure, love, and eroticism. Then we follow with Napoleon Bonaparte, who is considered one of the most iconic figures in world history. Although little about this is mentioned in the United States, Napoleon played a very important role not only in the independence of Mexico, but also his impact is directly reflected in various aspects of Mexican culture.

Violets were a distinctive symbol in the life of the French Empress Joséphine and her husband Napoleon Bonaparte. It is said that when Napoleon married Joséphine, she carried violets in her wedding gown, and that, when she died, Napoleon had her gravestone covered in violets. Shortly before he was exiled, he is said to have picked flowers from her grave. After Napoleon died, those violets were found in a locket he always wore around his neck.

Flowers and fruits carry several different meanings of romantic and spiritual significance and have influenced our magic in many ways. One of the ways that captivates my heart are the stories that my great grandmother used to tell me about when she was younger: how people used to exchange messages through different flowers, how they used different colors as well, in some kind of elaborate courtship code when they were that "marriageable age." For example, in my great grandmother's days, each color rose had a different message. A red rose meant "you are a flame in my heart," while the white ones meant a pure and less passionate love towards the other party, and a yellow rose meant disdain and perfidy.

These messages were also interpreted by the place where their flowers were pinned. If someone put a flower in their hair, it means that the chaperone was distracted or it was cool with the courtier, so they had a way to taste their love more freely. If the flower was pinned in a place close to a woman's heart, it meant that she was ready to go to the next step. Sometimes the same flower could mean different things depending on the color of the bloom or the place this flower was located. Other meanings and correspondences were attributed to flowers, thanks to songs, legends, and family history.

La Flor de Azhar: Orange Blossom

Mexico's flower of love is certainly the *flor de Azahar*, or the orange blossom. *Azahar* comes from the Arabic *az-Zahar*, which means "white flower." This flower is characteristic of all Mexican brides, or at least all of them who still follow the customs, traditions, and the superstition full of magic that is used to achieve a successful marriage. In this moment, if you are Mexican or have Mexican heritage, I challenge you to go and check your family picture album. Look for your mother's or perhaps your grandmother's bridal picture. I'm pretty sure you're going to spot this type of flower somewhere, most likely in their hair or dress, but also probably in their bouquet.

These small white flowers, which have a sweet and evocative aroma, come from citrus trees such as lemons, limes, and oranges, among others. My grandmother used to tell me about the reason for random flowers in a bride's clothing and in all the magical works of those who wanted to achieve or formalize a good love.

Mexico's Arabic heritage can be traced back to the Moors, who invaded Spain in 711 and ruled for almost eight hundred years. Some classic magical ingredients used in Mexican magic were originally brought to Spain by the Moors, and then the Spanish brought them to Mexico. The Arabs/Moors were the ones who introduced this tradition to Europe. The Arabs used to adorn the heads of brides with orange blossoms, and this tradition was introduced with a beautiful folktale. The folktale was about a couple who were very in love, but had no chance of marrying each other, and how this tree was an ally that allowed them to be able to consummate their love.

It is known that orange trees were only owned by the royalty in Al-Andalus, what today we would call a class privilege reserved for an elite. One day, a minister from the Christian kingdoms north of the Iberian Peninsula was visiting the royal place and became fascinated by an orange tree that was blooming at that time. He was fascinated not only by its beauty, but because the smell was somehow magical and intoxicating. He attempted to bribe the royal gardener into selling him a shoot from the tree. He offered different things, including a small fortune, but the gardener was so afraid of the repercussions he could suffer if he was caught that he refused to give the ambassador the flowers that the ambassador loved so much. But the gardener's daughter didn't even think and accepted the bribe.

It never even crossed her mind that Al-Andalus was in political and religious conflict with the Christian kingdoms in the north. She was so in love that she did not care and took that risk, putting her life and her father's life in danger. She did it because her love did not have enough money for the dote. (The dote is a provision accorded traditionally by a husband or his family to the bride's family in case she becomes widowed, or he leaves her.) So, she sold a cutting to the minister in order to have money to give to her beloved so they could marry.

It is said that the gardener's daughter, on her wedding day, placed one of these flowers in her hair and her bouquet as a sign of gratitude to the tree that had helped her marry. To this day, orange blossoms are an essential detail for all young women who get married in Mexico. Normally they are worn as a tiara or a hair dress that adorns the heads of brides.

Orange blossoms are a symbol of eternal love, fertility, and good luck. Their main magical use is to give good luck to a just married couple or attract a lover for someone who is looking for a serious relationship and marriage.

The tradition in the north of Mexico is that there must be at least three orange blossoms in the bride's bouquet, and when the wedding celebration is over, two flowers must be picked and placed in a white bag along with anise and three cloves. The bag must then be buried in the marital home ensuring that the marriage lasts forever. The flowers in the bag don't have to be natural flowers. They can be an artificial representation of this flower or their blossoms.

You can use these flowers to make your own amulets to attract love. You can dry them and dress your candles, and a variety of other things. I personally use orange blossom cologne after a shower to relax and attract good luck.

Oranges

The citrus region of Nuevo León has great relevance for this state, since it represents the largest area of industrial and demographic development. The first record of citrus in this region dates to the colonization of Mexico, although, at that time, the fruits produced in the orchards were only for self-consumption and magic. A certain mystery surrounds those oranges, probably because they are very adaptable trees that tolerate a wide range of soil conditions. It may be because it is a tree that is one of the easiest to enjoy in the world. Its leaves contain an essence composed of limonene and linalool, among other fragrant substances. It owes its sedative, calming, anti-spasmodic, and light somniferous action to these substances.

Para Encontrar a Tu Media Naranja: To Find Your Better Half

Whether we like it or not, a lot of Mexican magic has to do with the use of the Spanish language. I know, Spanish is the language of the colonizer, but it is the language that the vast majority of Mexicans have learned, developed, and made their own during the last almost five hundred years, and after those five hundred years, the Spanish we speak has evolved so much that even other Spanish speakers in Latin America don't understand a lot of the words we use in Spanish that have a Nahuatl origin.

Our Spanish is Mexican Spanish, and it sounds very different from the original Spanish, or what we would call Castilian language, "the medieval Old Spanish." I know that this may seem extremely difficult, even triggering for the average Mexican-American. Even for myself, it really is challenging to translate a lot of prayers that rhyme beautifully in Spanish but then don't rhyme when I translate them into English. If I make them rhyme and have sequence in English, the prayer in question ends up not translating accurately.

Language and popular culture play a very important role when it comes to this love magic ingredient. Mexicans say many very meaningful expressions. Many such expressions have become so common and popular in Mexico, such as *Encontrar a tu media Naranja*, "find your better half," a phrase that has to do with love and "finding soulmates." Finding your "better half" means finding that person who complements you, not completes you, as you are already complete.

Ever since we were children, we associated oranges and lemons with love, one of the first songs we learned as children was *Naranja Dulce, Limon Partido* (Sweet Orange, Cut Lemon), which was a children's circle game. The truth is that oranges are a great ally for magic. This ritual that I share with you is extremely old as well as effective.

> *Sweet orange, bring me that special person who will complement me and walk together the path of our lives, help me find my better half. Sweet orange, you who know which souls should be together, you are my hope in this desperate situation, I want to share my life with someone who loves me, who respects me, and who cherishes me, bring me that person with your sweet magical powers so we can be together.*

Vanilla

Vanilla is a key ingredient in most love and friendship spells and recipes. The name vanilla comes from the Spanish word *vainilla*, which means "little *vaina* (pod)." Native to Mexico, vanilla is a flavoring that comes from the seed of the climbing tropical orchid. The first cultivators of vanilla were the Totonacs of Veracruz, Mexico. According to a Totonac legend, the orchid was born when a Totonac princess was beheaded along with her lover, whom she was forbidden to marry, when they decided to run away together into the jungle. Both their blood touched the ground, and then the vine of the tropical orchid grew. This was later immortalized for posterity in Papantla (northern Veracruz) with a magnificent sculpture that has this legend written on it by a poet born in that city named José de Jesús Núñez y Domínguez (1887-1959).

In Mexico, this impossible love story is the one that is believed to have given life to this aromatic plant. Vanilla is one of the best allies for love potions in Mexico, but I need to warn you about the fact that vanilla is very pricey because it grows only once a year in certain regions. Instead, you can totally use imitation vanilla extract, which is made from vanillin. Vanillin is a component that's synthesized chemically from a liquid obtained by distilling the resin from the guaiacum tree. You can use either pure vanilla extract or imitation. Mexican vainilla in its liquid form is perfect for love jars and love spells.

Amarre de los Siete Nudos: Seven Knots Amarre with Vanilla

The seven knot *amarre* is one of the most famous amarres in Mexico. There are even kits sold in the mercados with all the things that you need for this specific ritual. This amarre is famous as an effective way to bind and tie up someone to our will.

You will need:

- Red ribbon

- A heart milagro

- Scissors

- Your own sexual secretions

- Vanilla extract

- Your own perfume or cologne

- Red candle

- Saint Anthony and Saint Marta prayer stamps or images

- A clay plate

- Matches

On a Friday, take your red ribbon and cut it to a length of twenty inches. Wet it with your own sexual body fluids and the liquid vanilla extract. Once you have it ready, place the two prayer stamps or images under the clay plate and place the candle on top of them. Light the candle and say the following with every knot that is tied in the ribbon:

> *With this first knot, I tie you up and lock you up.*
>
> *With this second knot, I tie you to my will and you will not act in any way other than the way I want and allow you to act.*
>
> *With this third knot, I tie you and tie your love and hold it firmly, and only I will be able to untie it.*
>
> *With this fourth knot, I tie you and tie your head, your thoughts, so that I will always be in your mind.*
>
> *With this fifth knot, I tie you and I tie your soul, so that your soul is consecrated to love me.*
>
> *With this sixth knot, I tie you and I tie your heart, so it is always beating for me.*

During the seventh knot, you are going to close the ribbon and make a knot to tie it together, so it is a perfect circle. Say:

> *With the seventh knot, I tie you completely and I own your freedom, your acts, your will, your love, your thoughts, your soul, and your heart.*

Once you have it ready, put some of your perfume or cologne on the ribbon circle and place the circle around the candle until the candle is consumed. After adding your heart milagro to the ribbon, wear it as a bracelet on your dominant hand.

If you want to undo this amarre, take the bracelet, untie the knots, and burn it to ashes.

CHAPTER EIGHT

MEXICAN KITCHEN MAGIC

A Molinillo to Get Married

A molinillo (swizzle stick).

The word *molinillo* comes from the Nahuatl *moliniani*, which means to *menear* or shake. Molinillos are made of wood. They have a long handle and a series of rollers that move independently near the tip. The purpose of this device is to foam chocolate and help it dissolve in hot water or milk. To accomplish this, you take the handle of the grinder between your hands and begin to spin it rapidly back and forth.

Whether it's hot chocolate, *champurrado*, or *atole*, it is said that it is better if you mix them with this pre-Hispanic invention.

A molinillo is something that cannot be missing in every Mexican kitchen, and in addition to having functions as practical as stirring, it is also believed to have esoteric powers related to love. It is said that if you want to get married soon, you should gift a newlywed couple a molinillo and a dowry of chocolate. This belief originated back in 1600 when Princess Anne married the Spanish King Louis XIII. Among the gifts she was given were pulverized cocoa and a molinillo gifted by another princess who got married immediately after. That story was brought to Mexico and a lot of women started to implement that magical tradition as an infallible gift to get married soon.

El Molinillo: Spice Up Your Sex Life

Chaca chaca is Mexican slang for naughty and kinky kinds of sex. Chaca chaca literally translates to *menea menea,* or to "shake shake." In Mexico it is believed that *si tu quieres chaca chaca deberas poner un molinillo debajo de tu cama,* or "if you want chaca chaca, you must hide a molinillo under your bed."

The Molinillo: The Wedding Checker

Mexican families are characterized by finding countless reasons to marry people. Who among us has not been the victim of the famous and very folkish Mexican kitchen comment: *ya te puedes casar* (you can get married)? Those are words that you heard from someone (usually elders) when you cooked something nice. A few centuries ago, when they wanted to verify that a person was ready to get married, that person was made to do the grinder test. The grinder test was that, when preparing chocolate, those people who managed to get a good foam with the help of a molinillo are ready to walk down the aisle and tie the knot.

La Ultima Cena So There Is No Lack of Bread on the Table

The Last Supper is one of the most famous religious-themed paintings, and it is present in the home of almost every Mexican family. It is placed in the kitchen or near the dining room table, not only for aesthetic purposes, but for magical, mystical purposes as well. I bet that Leonardo da Vinci would never have imagined the all-time trend of *The Last Supper* in Mexican homes. If you want to make sure that none of your family members gets sick, loses a job, suffers from economic needs, and is always protected, this ritual is for you.

You will need:

- A framed Last Supper painting
- Twelve *billetes* (paper money) of any denomination
- Tape
- *Aceite de proteccion* oil
- Abre caminos oil
- A little piece of *bolillo* (a type of bread)
- A white candle

On a Thursday, light a white candle with a lot of faith and trust that this ritual is going to be effective.

Grab your abre caminos oil and rub a little of it on every billete, focusing on the well-being of your home and every person who lives in it. Turn *The Last Supper* painting around so the back faces you and tape a billete on the body of every single apostle. Tape the little piece of bolillo on the back of the painting exactly where Jesus Christ sits. Rub the frame with aceite de proteccion oil.

Hang the painting in your kitchen or on the wall behind your dinner table. (The painting doesn't need to be huge like your grandma's picture frame. That is optional.) Once you hang the picture, repeat the following prayer twelve Thursdays in a row, including the Thursday that you hung your *Last Supper* painting.

> *Holy twelve men, holy twelve friends of God, I ask the twelve of you, for your holy protection, so that we do not lack housing, food, and sustenance for all of us who live inside here.*

> *O Lord Almighty, you who have given your twelve apostles power and virtues, I ask your twelve their divine intercession so that they can protect this home and take care of our health and our income and do not allow us to be the victim of spells, incantations or curses, unemployment, lack of faith, or gossip.*

> *May family peace and daily blessings always reign in this home today and always through the divine intercession of you the twelve apostles.*

> *Amen.*

Coffee

It is no surprise that coffee is considered the third most consumed beverage in the country and is present in 97 percent of Mexican homes. The accessibility and versatility that these beans offer have made it the ideal ingredient for many people who make spells with what they have on hand in their kitchen.

Café de la olla opens the door to the magical experience of connecting with our ancestors. The experience of living and feeling magic in the mundane is one of the greatest challenges for people nowadays when we try to pass what we experience as spirituality based on the logic of the extraordinary to a mysticism within the everyday. Our ancestors are always around. Yes, even in the kitchen, even on tumultuous mornings. Every morning I feel the strength of the spirit and the caress of my ancestors; when grinding the coffee, when serving it steaming in the cup, it connects me to the place where they saw me born, the call that I experience when my nose can smell the cloves and anise, the sweetness of my grandmothers when my palate tastes the *piloncillo* dulce and the orange peel, and the magical vapor coming out of my mug. My morning coffee is more than just a morning coffee. It is a way to feel them, touch them, and invite them.

One of the phrases that I find most inspiring about Santa Teresa de Avila is this: "Those whom the spirit brings to certain clear knowledge, love differently."

I never understood this phrase until a few years ago when I went to visit my son at his military base in Norfolk, Virginia. I understood that when the spirit brings a person to a certain clear knowledge, that person loves in a different way, because the spirit gave them the ability to love through space and time, even from another plane, another realm. They acquire the ability to hug and caress, even if they are not physically here with us, and I did not learn this lesson by carrying a very heavy suitcase full of tamales in three different airports, from Texas to Virginia during Christmas Eve madness. I witnessed this when my son tried his first tamale, that Christmas morning, and right after he chewed the first bite, he said, "Mom, I feel my Grandmother Diana is here with us." And make no mistake, she passed away in 2019. Those tamales were not made by my grandmother.

Our ancestors are like that. They live everywhere and their way of staying around is through things we keep doing every day. Their love leaves its trace; it does not follow our rules of time, space, present, past, or future. Magic happens when we stop trying to experience mysticism in very elaborate Hollywood-type situations and we start listening to the message now.

This coffee always helps me to connect with my ancestors. I do this mostly during the mornings on Mondays, then I offer them some copal resin.

El Café de Olla para Conectar con los Ancestros: Mexican Spiced Coffee in a Pot to Connect with Ancestors

At the beginning of the 18th century, coffee was an imported product in the New World. It first arrived in Haiti, where there are records of its cultivation in 1715. In Veracruz's port, it can be traced back to 1790. At the same time, spices with a marked influence of the flavors of the Middle East arrived due to the Arab occupations in their territory.

It wasn't until the early twentieth century that *café de olla* was born. It was during the Mexican Revolution, where women made their mark on the frontlines, that it was created to keep up the morale of the soldiers and keep them awake. These women created a blend of spices, coffee, and sugar in clay pots which they would then hand out to all the soldiers for comfort and an energy boost. This blend of coffee would be called café de olla, literally meaning "coffee from a clay pot."

De la olla coffee is very traditional. It is made with Mexican ground coffee, cinnamon, and raw dark sugar that we call piloncillo, as well as anise, cloves, and orange peel. This is a traditional Mexican drink recipe that has been enjoyed by many generations! If you are trying to connect with your ancestors, even if they are not Mexican, it is an excellent offering. I am pretty sure they are going to be delighted. Think of café de la olla like a potent medicine to heal your relationship with your ancestors and your lineage, if you have something you need to heal. You can use this coffee as an offering as well.

You will need only a cup of café de olla, a picture of your ancestors, and this prayer to start the dialogue.

Ingredients for café de olla:

4 cups water

1/2 cup packed piloncillo

2 medium cinnamon sticks

2 anise seeds

2 whole cloves

1 pinch of dry orange peal

3 to 4 tablespoons Nescafe Clasico Instant Coffee granules

Combine water, piloncillo, cinnamon sticks, anise, and cloves in medium saucepan. Heat over medium-high heat, stirring occasionally, until boiling. Reduce heat to low, cover. Cook for ten minutes. Remove from heat and stir in coffee granules. Cover and steep for ten minutes. Heat half and half creamer in small saucepan over medium-high heat. Whisk constantly until it is frothy and just comes to a boil. Remove from heat. Strain coffee through a fine sieve into individual serving cups. Serve immediately with warmed up half and half on the side (optional).

Prayer to the Ancestors

Beloved Ancestors, the ones who came before me, the ones who had the opportunity to live, those who were not born. The dreamers. The lovers. The excluded and secluded. The ones who were invisible. The ones who emigrated. For which his spirit continues to accompany me. Those that continue shining. The pioneers.

This morning, I bless my entire family lineage, and I honor my ancestors of my previous generations: parents, grandparents, great-grandparents, great-great-grandparents . . . who paved the way to make my presence possible on this plane of existence, in this perfect moment. I thank and bless your walk and your inheritance of wisdom and magic for my own walk. Likewise, I honor and bless all my ancestors and descendants who are still alive and the next generations in my family to come. This morning I especially honor all those women who came before me, all the immigrant grandmothers, great-grandmothers, great-great-grandmothers, who with their effort, love, struggle, and persever-ance, did what they could with the resources they had at that time to be able to get ahead in this country despite the limitations and their language barrier. I honor their sacrifices, their suffering, their work because none of it was in vain. I'm thankful for you and your example.

Thank you, thank you, thank you! Salud! Cheers!

To Force Someone to Tell the Truth

If you are trying to get someone to tell the truth, but this person is hiding it for some reason, there is a secret formula that works as a truth serum. With this ancient but powerful formula, you will be able to obtain information from subjects who are unable or unwilling to provide it otherwise.

This should be done during the day or evening before the sun goes down. It is enough to give the person coffee to drink made with holy water which you will boil with a sprig of thyme. Stir the contents from time-to-time counter-clockwise, that is, making circles to the left, and concentrate on what you want to know.

Once the coffee is ready, give it to the person to whom you will intel-ligently ask what you want to know. Allow this person to speak without interruptions.

To Kick Someone Out of Your Home

Coffee and tea are consumed when people are in need of a good break, or, in the case of a coffee, when our brain needs a kickstart, but what happens when you need a break from someone? Or when you need to kick out or drive an inconvenient person away from your home?

Offer this person a cup of coffee or tea with holy water from a church dedicated to San Alejo and it is a fact that the targeted person will leave your home. San Alejo (Saint Alexius) is the right saint to help you remove unwanted people from your home.

Las Aguas Frescas

Las Aguas frescas means "refreshing waters." Most aguas frescas are nonalcoholic beverages made from one or more fruits, cereals, flowers, or seeds, blended with raw sugar and water. Some of these aguas frescas are fermented and contain alcohol thanks to that fermentation, like the *tepache*. These waters are very popular in Mexico and part of every Mexican kitchen's repertoire of beverages.

El Agua de Jamaica

El agua de jamaica, which translates as "hibiscus water," is a typical agua fresca made to accompany a meal in Mexico. It is a delicious beverage that is unique to Mexican culture and even has numerous medicinal benefits, but also it has a lot of stories behind it. One such story among Mexican people is that this traditional agua fresca was the liquid of choice in which to hide the infamous *agua de calzón,* the panty water.

El Agua de Calzón: The Panty Water

This working is for when you need to dominate and control someone's behavior, life, and decisions, in the same way that we want someone to fall madly in love with us.

El agua de calzón translates to "panty water" in English, and it's a popularly known domination tool in Mexico. The agua de calzón is a type of potion that could be classified as a dominion, since the aim of this procedure is to make your partner submissive towards you. Despite being popularly known, very few people know the original and powerfully effective recipe. In addition to controlling your target, this potion is going to make the person who drinks it unknowingly fall in love with you and feel an instant attraction and romantic desire.

The preparation of agua de calzón is very simple.

You will need:

- A pair of underwear that you have worn overnight after taking a bath

- 1250ml of purified water (a little over five cups)

- 15g of hibiscus flowers

- Brown sugar

- A pot

- A pitcher

When the underwear has been worn overnight, the fabric is impregnated with the sweat and the pheromones of the person who wore it. Pheromones are associated with sexual attraction, as well as being a chemical signal of recognition and domination. In addition, hibiscus is considered not only an aphrodisiac but a miracle worker in the flower world.

Bring the water to a boil in a pot and, once it is boiling, immerse the panty in the water. Add in hibiscus flowers and stir for one minute before removing them. Add brown sugar to taste; some people like their agua de Jamaica bitter and some like it very sweet. Strain it and let the water cool overnight. Now all you have to do is get your target (usually your man) to drink the water.

La Horchata Baño for Financial Prosperity

Do you need a little help attracting more money into your life? This *baño* (bath) is easy to make and requires only rice and a few other items that you probably already have at home. Learn to do it step by step and start attracting the prosperity you deserve.

Horchata (pronounced or-*chah*-tah) is a popular Mexican drink that is often described as a rice beverage (*agua de arroz*). Although it's a simple concoction, this drink has healing and magical properties, and it can be used as a baño spiritual. A spiritual bath is intended to clean, purify, and eliminate negativity that is holding back, blocking, or affecting our body and our spirit. This particular baño combines ingredients that are capable of attracting luck, prosperity, and money into your life, in addition to raising your energy. If you are currently in a difficult economic situation or simply want to increase your financial solvency, I recommend that you try this as soon as possible.

You will need:

- 1 cup of rice
- 2/3 cup of sugar
- 2 cinnamon sticks
- 1 teaspoon vanilla extract
- 1 can evaporated milk
- 1.5 cups of milk or almond milk
- A large bowl or a *tina* (bucket)

If you don't already have these ingredients, don't worry. They are all easy to find and inexpensive.

You must soak the rice and cinnamon in water for an extended period. That is so that you can ensure that all the magical properties have seeped into the water. The best way to do this is to start soaking the ingredients the night before your bath, preferably during a waxing crescent moon for prosperity. That way, you can set intentions and have a good night's sleep instead of just standing around waiting for this magical baño to be ready!

Once you have soaked the ingredients all night long and set your financial goals and intentions, the next steps are easy. Blend the cinnamon and the rice mixture with evaporated milk until a smooth mix is formed and the grains of rice are completely ground. Strain the resulting liquid into a container, and add the sugar, vanilla, and milk. Mix until everything is well combined. Add this into a container so you can use it later for your bath. (You can refrigerate this mixture for three or four days.) It is ideal that you perform this financial prosperity bath at a time of day when you feel completely relaxed and fully confident that this bath will work. A good option is to do it at night before going to sleep. When you have your bathtub ready and it is at a comfortable temperature, add the mixture to the tub, and immerse yourself in the water for at least fifteen minutes. You can then continue your daily bathing routine as usual, so you do not finish your bath or shower all sticky from the sugar and the other ingredients.

If you do not have a bathtub, you can take the mixture into the shower. Just place the mixture in a spray container and, when it's time to shower, spray your body from head to toe with this powerful magical spray.

Cookies

In every culture, nothing reminds us of our abuelas' homes as much as cookies. Cookies in Mexican culture can be a great source of magic if you know where to find them: butter cookies containers.

El Dominio con Almohadas Mágicas

The origins of pincushions date back to the Middle Ages in Europe. This artifact is a stuffed piece of fabric that you can insert pins into; most likely your grandma had at least one of them. Our Mexican grandmothers were really good at hiding their brujeria, and one of those unexpected hiding places was their Danish butter cookie containers that they repurposed as sewing kits. Inside of these tins, they always had magical pincushions.

Those pincushions may seem harmless, but for generations they have been an efficient and easily concealed medium for the magical work of domination, combining the power of certain herbs, pictures, and prayers with which these pincushions can be filled. One of the most infallible works of domination was taught to me by Dona Fatima, a seamstress by trade, who had five daughters who were "really lucky" in that they married very well-off and powerful men when they didn't belong to the same social class, or even the same circle of friends. All these women knew how to get into the heart and the five senses of a man in the old-fashioned way, just like a thread through a needle.

For this trabajo, you will need:

- Red cotton fabric (fat quarters are better)

- Polyester stuffing

- Needle

- Red thread

- Scissors

- Ruler

- Fabric marker

- Heart-shaped stencil

- Picture of your target

- Five sewing pins

- Cinnamon

- Dried red rose petals

- Lavender

Trace two equal-sized heart shapes onto your red fabric and cut them out. You can trace these onto the fabric using a fabric marker, or, if you don't have one, a ballpoint pen. Then cut along the lines using a pair of sharp fabric scissors.

Place the fabric hearts together so that their right (print or front) sides are facing each other. (You want the back or unprinted side to face outwards.) Sew a straight stitch around the outside of the hearts about 0.25 inches from the edges. Stop about 1.5 inches from the opening, leaving a gap.

Cut off the excess threads at the beginning and end of the seam. Use the shears to trim around the outside of the fabric.

Use your fingers and the back of a pencil or chopstick to invert the fabric so that the seam is hidden, and the right side of the fabric is visible. Push stuffing in through the opening in the seam.

In the middle of the stuffing, you are going to add a picture of your target, cinnamon, dry red rose petals, and lavender.

Thread a needle and hand sew the opening closed. Once it is closed, repeat the following prayer and place into the pin cushion one pin every time you mention a sense, forming a cross shape with those pins.

> *In the name of the Lord Almighty*
>
> *Here are the five senses that I want to dominate in (target's name) in the present and in the future. That every time I see (target's pronouns) sees back at me. That every time I speak (target's pronouns) listens to me. That every time my hands want to touch (target's pronouns) caresses me. That every time I breathe (target's pronouns) sighs for me.*
>
> *So, my five senses are pinned to (target's pronouns) heart today and forever, by God in the same place at the same time.*
>
> *Amen.*

Cookies Maria: Las Galletas Marías

This working is done so money arrives, reaches you immediately, and yields triple.

A situation that manifested itself constantly in the construction of traditional recipes, and one that goes hand in hand with modernization in the kitchen and in magic, is the incorporation of processed products. Some products in particular stand out: flour corn (Maseca and Maicena brand), wheat flour, crackers, Galletas Marías, and vegetable lard shortening (Inca brand).

Maria cookies are very popular in all Mexican pantries; without a doubt, this is something that is never lacking, especially if you have small children. They can be stacked in a Carlota lemon dessert, eaten with *cajeta,* with jam, or alone to *chope* (dip) in a coffee or milk. It can be said that most Mexicans were raised eating these cookies. Babies love them, and they are extremely economical and a delight to the palate. *The Encyclopedic Dictionary de la Gastronomía Mexicana* explains that these cookies, which are sold by various brands in Mexico, originate from Europe. However, when they arrived in Mexico, they became so popular that many believe they were born in our country. Maria cookies arrived in Mexico thanks to the Gamesa company, who took the recipe from a Catalan family recently arrived in Monterrey, Nuevo León. Since their creation, a Maria cookie has been a symbol of economic recovery, creativity, and resourcefulness.

If you are struggling financially, buy at least one package of Maria cookies. Separate three cookies and wet them with rainwater, then sprinkle the cookie crumbs on the patio of your house or in front of your business. Do this on a Sunday very early in the morning, somewhere birds can eat the crumbs. Look at the sky and ask it that, just like cookies attract these birds, so easy and simply will you attract and triple your money.

Galletas Marias are not a complete food for wild birds and do not provide adequate nutrition for mature birds or young birds. They may snack on that type of food from time to time but not on a regular basis. Therefore, this ritual should be done only once a year.

Mexican Candy

There are a wide variety of typical Mexican sweets that you have hopefully tried and fallen in love with the flavor. It does not matter if you prefer sour, sweet, or savory, because there is something for all tastes. Traditional sweets in Mexico are a great magical resource, not only for offerings on our altars, but because confectionery is also part of our heritage, culture, and magical repertoire.

La Virgen de la Dulce Espera: Expectation of the Blessed Virgin Mary

Many Mexican women establish their faith in Our Lady of the Sweet Wait to ask for the blessing of a child, especially when they find it difficult to conceive. In the same way, we turn to her to express the joy of a pregnancy, to ask her for the birth of a new healthy being, and, finally, to thank her once the baby is born. There are many prayers and rituals asking and giving thanks to her for the favors received. Among the popular magical rituals that are performed, this is one of the most predominant.

To ask for the miracle of conceiving a child or carrying your pregnancy to term, you will have to steal a sock from a baby and fill it with Mexican candy. Take it to your altar or to a church with a Marian dedication and ask her with all your faith that you become a mother.

December 18th is the established date to celebrate the *Virgen de la Dulce Espera*. The next following year after your request is fulfilled and you have had your baby, you will thank her by offering a second sock filled with Mexican candy. This time the sock will be from your own baby.

Chicles: Chewing Gum

Chicles are one of the top candies in Mexico. Chewing gum has existed since pre-Hispanic times, but not as we know it today. Chewing gum has changed and evolved, but its soft and sticky consistency has remained, along with a tasty flavor added by the companies that produce it. As Mexicans, we have a very traditional magical use for chewing gum.

To Stop Gossip, Slander, and Libel

San Ramon (Saint Raymond), whose feast day is August 31, is the patron saint of expectant mothers, infertility issues, and travelers. But he also is a saint whose intercession is especially helpful to people in Mexico seeking to stop the *habladurias, chismes,* and *calumnias* (gossip, slander, and libel).

Buy an image of the saint, such as a prayer stamp or statue. You can even print a picture at home. Stick a coin either in or over the mouth with Campeche wax or any chewing gum that you chew yourself and repeat:

> *"San Ramon, ponle en la boca un tapón."* Saint Raymond put a plug in (person's name) mouth.

> *San Ramón Nonato (Saint Raymond), you who for preaching the word of God carried a padlock in your mouth martyrdom, listen to my prayer and intercede before God so that those who speak ill of me cease their intent and I be protected from all evil words and intentions. Amen.*

The coin stuck in the mouth and the gum is left indefinitely until the gossip, chismes, and habladurías stops.

Also, if you are in front of the person who gets you into chismes, you can say in a low voice or mentally: "San Ramon, make sure (person's name or pronouns) shuts up." With this you will begin to silence them.

Amarres

Traditional amarres are one of the main reasons I started writing about Mexican brujeria, hechicería, and magia. I know for a fact that we can get lost in translations and the meanings of said translations. I have seen often that a lot of books on Mexican magic and witchcraft in the US reduce what an amarre means in the Mexican sense and totally leave aside the historical and religious connotations from pre-Hispanic times.

An amarre is more than a "love spell." It is actually a ritual. This ritual is an imitative form of marriage ceremonies in Mexico, a symbolic and magical representation of two people becoming one in marriage. First, there's the amarre de *tilma* and *huipil* (mooring of tilma and huipil), which was performed to unite Mexican couples in marriage, and the wedding lasso tradition in the Catholic church. In both ceremonies, that "knot" kept the couple tied and symbolized their perpetual union and status as one.

There is abundant cultural context behind this traditional and iconic practice. With that being said, there is one material absolutely required for amarres to be traditional: cords, laces, rope, ribbon, or anything that can be used to tie, knot, or bind. Just as every person who enters a marriage doesn't enter under the same circumstances and intentions, not every amarre is created with the same goals. Some amarres are very infamous and the ingredients that are used are picked to restrain, dominate, and enforce submission. This type of amarre usually comes with sensory deprivation, like adding blindfolds as a way to exert our control. Insomnia so the person cannot think clearly, loss of appetite, and restlessness are induced through certain ingredients, traditional conjures, and prayers. On the other hand, there are amarres that push a marriage for more benevolent reasons and rely on other types of ingredients.

Amarre with Chocolate Carlos V

This was the first amarre I did when I was young, a couple of months before I started high school. This amarre was not for me; it was for one of my cousins who used to pick me up from school. She was in a very long relationship (five years) but, for some reason, her boyfriend was afraid to take the next step. Amarres are the best way to push magically for marriages.

This amarre is perfect for people who have very little experience with magic or who are not able to spend a fortune on materials. It is simple, but make no mistake, this amarre is very efficient.

Chocolate has long played a leading role in Mexico. Our ancestors' use of cacao varies greatly, but chocolate has a lot of properties that generate a range of different feelings between lovers; in fact, it drives and intensifies those feelings. That is why chocolate bars are the best material for this amarre. If you are Mexican or have Mexican friends, you know that Carlos V chocolate is very famous due to its sweet flavor and affordable price. You can find it everywhere, from convenience stores to pharmacies.

You will need:

- Two Carlos V chocolate bars

- A red ribbon

- A personal item belonging to the person you want to tie to you (in case you are doing this working for someone else, you need a personal belonging from each of them, preferably hair, nail clippings, or a little fabric cut from their clothes)

- A tiny mason jar or a clean baby food jar

- One white candle

- A wooden toothpick

- A plate

On a Friday night, grab the two chocolate bars and open them. With your toothpick, write the name of the targets, one name in one bar and the other name in the second bar. Place the bars one on top of the other, uniting them on the flat side. Tie them together with the red ribbon. Place the personal belongings in the empty mason jar.

Melt the chocolate bars together. You can choose the method, but I highly recommend a bain-marie. When using a bain-marie, the temperature rises gradually and never reaches or exceeds 100°C, making it the ideal method for melting things like chocolate. Keep the ribbon tied around them.

Pour the melted chocolate and the ribbon inside of the jar. You can use a spoon in case it gets thick. Put the lid on the jar. Place the candle on top of the jar and light it. Once the candle is burning, repeat the following prayer:

> *I call upon the loving virtues of these sacred seeds, so (here say the names of the targets) may unite in love, trust, and happiness. Unify their lives, make them one, like fused chocolate. May the flame of this love get as strong as the flame of this candle that I light tonight, so in this way they stay together, from now and forever.*
>
> *So be it and so it will be.*

Santa Marta Amarres in Colonial and Contemporary Magic

Saint Martha of Bethany (Santa Marta) was the sister of Lazarus and Mary. Her feast is commemorated on July 29th. It is not surprising that with the arrival of Iberian and African magic to what we now call Latin America, Santa Marta was the most requested saint for amarres. It makes a lot of sense since Santa Marta is the patron saint of housewives, homemakers, and service woman. In addition, the legend says that the saint enchanted, tied up, dominated, and subdued a beast. The beast stood meek while Saint Martha tied him up with her girdle, which is pretty much what a lot of women wanted to accomplish with their man. Still to this day she's prayed to when a woman wants to bind and dominate a man.

Just like Saint Martha, every Mexican woman, even in modern times, is tired, culturally burdened with much serving, anxious, and troubled about many things. It's important to highlight that Martha la Dominadora within the Hoodoo practice, Voodoo, and other Afro-Caribbean religious traditions (mainly spiritualism and the 21 Divisions) is not the same as Martha la Mala (the Wicked Martha) in Mexican magic. Take into consideration that there exist different manifestations of the same saints due to the location and the culture of origin, although they share many of the same virtues and patronages.

Saint Martha Amarre for Marriage

You will need:

- Two dolls or poppets (I highly recommend using a bride and groom cake topper from a wedding)
- A flower from a bridal bouquet
- One green ribbon to represent Santa Marta's girdle (the thicker the better)
- A permanent marker
- A Santa Marta or red candle

On a Friday night, write the name of each person on the back of the figures, one on one figure and the second on the other, with permanent marker. Place the flower from the bridal bouquet between them.

Take the two dolls and the flower in the middle and tie everything together with the green ribbon. Make three turns and three knots so that the bride and groom will be tied in marriage. Then put this amarre in velacion (candlelight) with a Santa Marta candle and pronounce the following words:

> *I invoke you, the Wicked Marta, the unholy, the subduer,*
> *and the matchmaker, the one with whom a hundred devils dance.*
> *Wicked Marta, you who subdue a dragon at your feet and binds*
> *the passions between men and women, I ask you to bring me as*

husband/wife (name of the target) and tie (target's pronouns) to me for the rest of (target's pronouns) life. Oh, glorious Saint Martha, may this be a good marriage full of commitment and love, may your girdle allow me to bind and control my beloved today and forever, may your torch ignite my beloved with passion and lust.

Amen.

Salt: To Avoid Salaciones and Bad Luck in Your Kitchen

According to Mexican beliefs, salt brings bad luck and should not be spilled on the table. Throwing salt is an omen of bad luck for the one who throws it, and even worse for the ones next to them. This is because it is said that, at the last supper of Jesus Christ, Judas threw the salt, hence the expression *ya te salaste*. If the salt is spilled, it should be caught with the left hand and thrown back over the right shoulder.

In the same manner, among Mexicans, when requesting a salt shaker, you *should never* say "pass me the salt," "give me the salt," or "hand me the salt," because this causes the person requesting it and handling it to have bad luck, that is, *salarte*. Instead, salt should be placed in the center of Mexican kitchen tables to avoid bad luck.

Potatoes to Remove Salt from Your Home

The potato (*papa blanca*) was not known during the pre-Hispanic period in Mexico. However, shortly after the Conquest, it was cultivated in massive quantities, which is why it became part of the diet and cuisine in all the states of Mexico. Its use gave rise to an endless series of fundamental and very traditionally Mexican stews. Since then, this inexpensive and very versatile tuber has been used in many types of food, from *picadillo con papas* to *tacos de canasta*.

The potato has many practical and magical virtues, but one of the most important, both in cooking and in Mexican magic, is its ability to remove excess salt. If you prepare a soup or stew and it is a little salty, add sliced potatoes and leave them for a few minutes. The potato will absorb the excess salt.

If you want to remove salt, be it from your life, your home, or your finances, perhaps because you feel that you are going through more unfortunate events than normal, or maybe your plans are not going as you expect, and you feel your environment is especially salty, put a peeled potato in a glass of clean water and place it behind the entryway door. It will attract salt and prevent salting in your home or place of business. Change the potato and water daily and discard the potato away from your home or place of business.

To Prevent Indigestion, Brujeria, or Ill Intent in Food

For Mexicans, it is important that, when adding spices when cooking, it is always done in the shape of a cross. When putting in salt, it is also important to do it like this. This way, people do not get indigestion. In case you have not prepared your food yourself, bless it with the sign of the cross.

Traditional Tea to Cure Brujeria Ingested Through Food

It is well known that a recurring practice in Mexico is adding witchcraft to food. This brujeria can be very hard to notice and can come in any form or shape, although usually powders. For this reason, people must be careful what they eat or drink and with whom they eat or drink it. Often the same friends, relatives, and coworkers, people with whom we have some kind of relationship, lend themselves to transport, offer, or add brujeria into our food or drinks.

This tea is the best *corta* brujeria to sip after any suspicion of brujeria in your food, and it is very easy to make.

You will need:

   3 cups of water

   3 Mexican lemons (the green ones, not the yellow ones) cut halfway
      into each lemon in a cross-shaped pattern

   3 cloves

   1 tablespoon of dried crushed *boldo* leaves or a boldo tea bag.

Combine all ingredients in a pot and simmer for ten to twelve minutes. Allow it to steep for another ten minutes.

While you wait, repeat the following prayer and focus on the healing of the bewitched.

> *Healing Spirit of the boldo, the lemon, and the nails with which our Lord Jesus Christ was crucified, heal the body, the soul, and the spirit of (name of the bewitched), of all evil work of witchcraft in what (name of the bewitched) has ingested and that entered (pronouns of the bewitched) body without (bewitched's pronouns) knowing, in the name of the Father, the Son, and the Holy Spirit.*
>
> *Amen.*

Strain before serving. Do not sweeten.

Sugar Bath

The sugar bath is an excellent purifier to wash the soul, the heart, and the mind of all the bad feelings that you keep inside your being. If you feel heavy due to negative energies, you can count on the power of sugar to cleanse your physical body and spirit. In addition, the sugar bath is known for its power to open paths of sweetness and attract love and friendship into your life. You can carry out this ritual whether you are looking for love or simply want to attract sincere friends with good intentions into your life.

The sugar bath is also used in the following situations:

- When you start a new job

- When you move house or place of residence

- After a love or friendship breakup

- When you have a desire for revenge because someone did you wrong

- When you feel alone because you don't have someone by your side

We must not forget that sugar, in addition to attracting sweetness, is a protective shield against the bitterness of others towards our lives. Sugar is a great, powerful, and accessible ally in difficult times.

You will need:

- A white candle

- 1 cup of white sugar

- 3 liters of purified water

Begin the ritual by lighting the white candle and leave the other ingredients in *velacion* (candlelight) for at least three hours. Then, in a container, add the water, asking with good intentions that this water cleanse your body, your mind, and your spirit. Add the sugar to the container with your left hand, focusing and concentrating as you ask it now to sweeten your body, your spirit, you mind, and your path.

After bathing as usual with water, shampoo, and soap, pour the mixture all over your body, mentally projecting positive thinking and cleansing for your soul.

Finally, remove the excess sugar bath left on your skin with water and neutral soap and let your body dry on its own.

Bread

There is no self-respecting Mexican who does not love bread or who can live without it. Bread in any form (sweet or savory) cannot be missing in any traditional Mexican kitchen. Wheat was a great contribution from the Spanish to our diet, and bread, one of its most exquisite forms, is the traditional companion of our meals and snacks. Who can resist the bolillo, a vanilla or chocolate *concha*, or perhaps a just out of the oven *pan de los pobres*?

The magical, religious, and popular traditions of Mexico are reflected in the style of Mexican bakeries to this day. A perfect example is *el pan de dia de Muertos*, or the Day of the Dead bread, as well as the *Rosca de Reyes* (Three Kings Bread), which in Mexico gives its own touch of this tradition that came from Spain. The Mexican bakery is part of our culture and traditions. Mexico is the country with the greatest variety of bread, due to the heritage and culinary fusions that our gastronomy has experienced over the years since pre-Hispanic times, such as during the viceroyalty and then later with French and other influences in different regions of the country. The different types of bread in Mexico are foods that are part of a ritual. This ritual is accompanied by memories and nostalgia, by childhood, colors, stories, and flavors to drink with a cup of coffee.

El Pan de los Pobres para Pedir un Milagro: Saint Anthony Bread to Ask for a Miracle

This devotion to Saint Anthony dates to the 13th century and this tradition is a source of many favors and graces. It is of great help to people who are struggling with any issue, especially money matters.

According to a legend, while the great basilica was being built in Padua, a boy fell into a barrel of water and drowned. In her pain, the boy's mother asked Saint Anthony for help and promised that she would donate the child's weight in grain to the poor if he was brought back to life. While the mother was still praying, the boy got up as if he had just been sleeping. This miracle gave origin to the beautiful and magical practice of giving alms to the poor as a request or in exchange for favors received through the intercession of Saint Anthony.

There is a very Mexican and traditional recipe for this bread. The recipe differs in every state. This recipe was shared with me by a beautiful abuelita from Michoacan. The preparation of this bread is similar and comparable to that of other types of savory bread that are made in Mexico; what makes this bread magical and special is sharing it with others and the faith you put in the process.

  1/2 kg all purpose flour
  25 g fresh yeast
  2 teaspoons of salt
  1 teaspoon of sugar
  2 tablespoons olive oil
  250 ml of water

Mix the flour with salt and sugar and reserve a handful of flour. Dissolve the yeast in warm water. Form a volcano and add the rest of the ingredients in the center. Then knead the dough for ten minutes.

When it has doubled in volume, cut 60 g portions. Shape the rolls in the way you like best and let them rest on a tray with parchment paper. Cover them with a cloth for twenty minutes. The *bollitos*, or round loaves, must be flattened by hand or with a rolling pin, as if we were making a ball as round as possible.

After twenty minutes, make some small cross-shaped cuts and let the loaves rest for about forty more minutes, covered with the cloth, until they double their volume. Preheat the oven to 200°C, paint the buns with the mixture of water and oil, and bake for ten minutes. Lower to 180°C and bake for ten more minutes, or until golden brown.

To ask for a miracle, offer San Antonio that you will bake these delicious little breads and distribute them among your friends and family, and those who most need this type of blessing. In case you are not very endowed with grace and virtue in the kitchen, it may be more practical to offer Saint Anthony instead that you will give alms or donations as payment for your requested miracle. Alms to San Antonio in Mexico are usually helping the families of migrants, economic contributions to widows and orphans, homeless people, nursing homes, and other charitable causes.

San Cayetano el Santo del Trabajo

San Cayetano (Saint Cajetan) is patron saint of the unemployed and job seekers. He is called Father of Providence, and he is also the patron saint of bread. He was known as a very generous soul since he gave up his luxurious lifestyle and dedicated his life to the poor, job seekers, and the unemployed. With his own resources, he established a bank to shield the poor from exploitation by the loan sharks of his time. The Italian presbyter gave himself to austerity in order to help the ones in need. His legacy has been remembered since his death on August 7, 1547. August 7 is his feast day.

San Cayetano, bendiceme con pan y trabajo.

Saint Cajetan, bless me with bread and a well-paid job.

This magical recipe will ensure there is no lack of daily bread on the table and that you get a well-remunerated job, sales, or any endeavor that will help you to support yourself and your family.

You will need:

- A bolillo
- Olive oil
- Gold acrylic paint
- Glue
- 3 wheat sticks
- A San Cayetano prayer stamp or image
- A small brush

On a Wednesday, take the piece of bread and proceed to paint it with gold acrylic paint. Once it has dried, verify that the bread is completely golden in color. Make a small hole in the top of the bread and nail the three sticks of wheat, one by one, saying:

Oh, glorious San Cayetano, Father of Providence! That your generous hand aid me, I ask to you in the earthly and the spiritual.

Glue the image or San Cayetano prayer stamp on the wheat sticks and bless it with the olive oil: with your fingers anointed in the oil, make the sign of the cross on the bottom of the bread.

Finish this recipe by saying this prayer with lots of faith:

San Cayetano, my dear friend and intercessor, today I come to ask you for help, so that you intercede for me and help me find a well-paid job, and that you help me keep it despite adverse circumstances and people, that in my new job I can develop my gifts and talents, improving my lifestyle and that of those I love, I thank you in advance for your prompt help and I promise to spread this devotion today and forever.

Amen.

Place this bread in your pantry or wherever you keep your dry food and cans.

Marranitos Bread for Overall Goodness, Abundance, and Prosperity

Marranitos (piggy-shaped pan dulce) are a sweet bread made from flour, cinnamon, dark brown sugar, and unsulfured molasses, and can be found in any Mexican bakery. It is believed that if you have them on your kitchen table, you will never lack money and sweetness in your home. The bread remains, at least in our Mexican culture, a powerful symbol of the rudimentary basis of provision for our needs.

Divination with Fava Beans

The most common divination methods in Mexico are methods related to cooking or easy to hide in our cupboards. They're easy to hide because they have common uses in our day-to-day lives. One of these divination methods arrived during the times of the Conquest. Colonial sorceresses possessed a magical repertoire of different origins. Iberian influences were notable, arriving with Spanish and Portuguese women who came to reside in different cities of the viceroyalty of New Spain, what we call Mexico nowadays. In addition, many important African and Sephardic Jewish influences came across to nourish and blend with indigenous magic beliefs. These beliefs survived thanks to oral tradition and Inquisitorial texts.

One of the greatest examples of syncretism in divinatory practice is *las habas* (the fava beans). This method consists of gathering fava beans with other pieces, shaking them in our hands, and then throwing them on the floor or on a tablecloth. The fava bean reading is an intuitive method with certain characteristics, which varied greatly from place to place in Mexico.

Even though this practice is of Iberian origin, in the times of the colonization it started to acquire elements of the New World.

You will need:

- Red sachet
- Black bandana
- 7 fava beans
- Alum stone
- A coin
- A rock
- A tiny obsidian stone
- A tiny turquoise stone
- A hard piece of bread
- A red thread
- A key
- A grain of coffee
- A piece of paper
- A white candle

On a Friday night, gather all the items together, light the candle, and offer a glass of water to the spirits. After you have everything ready, place the seven fava beans inside of your mouth and hold them there for a couple of minutes. Spit them one by one on top of the black bandana, where you have already gathered the rest of the ingredients. Say the following conjure:

Fava beans, that between heaven and earth you were sown, and with dew from heaven you were sprinkled, just as this is true, it will be true that you are going to answer the questions that I'm going to ask to you.

I conjure Saint Peter, Saint Paul, Saint James, with the holy house of Rome, with the creatures, with the oceans, the sky, the sands, the heavens, and hell, and with the virtues that are in them, give me the answer for what I'm going to ask.

The seven fava beans represent a character in the reading. You can mark them with symbols or letters.

- God

- The devil

- Ourselves (or the person to whom the reading is dedicated)

- A man

- A woman

- A second man

- A second woman

The alum stone means banishing, clearing, getting rid of something, walking away.

The coin represents wealth, earthly possessions, money, profit, but like everything else we need to analyze if the coin is close to the devil, which would mean ill-gotten money, ruin, bankruptcy, or corruption.

The obsidian stone represents the night, hidden situations, trickery, cunning, ancestors, the shadow self, war, sharp objects, and hostility.

The stale bread means life, transformation, pregnancy, continuity, traditions, manifestation, blessings, nourishments, creation, and process.

The red thread means the cord of life, destiny, entanglement, amarres, or a leash.

The meanings of the key vary depending on where the other items are placed on the reading. The key can mean opening doors to the spirit or celestial realms, or higher hierarchy or society circles, or it could mean the opposite. If it is close to the obsidian, that would mean a big secret. If it is close to God, it could mean opening roads.

The coffee grain means quick or bitter situations to come.

The piece of paper suggests letters, contracts, legal matters, study.

The rock means paths, roads, travel, strength, but also the lack of feelings towards one person.

The turquoise stone represents the day, the sun, royalty, legacy, metamorphosis, transition.

Instructions:

Hold the fava beans and the other elements with your two hands, four inches above the center of the black bandana or casting cloth. Ask your questions, either silently or out loud.

Carefully release all the elements, but do not throw them. Note where they have landed.

Check what elements are touching each other, which ones are close or completely far away from each other. Check which ones are in opposition or if one element is on top of another element.

Read the appropriate message. Place all the elements gently in the bandana and make a knot to finish.

The Messy Kitchen Drawer

In a typical Mexican kitchen, there is always a drawer of miscellaneous items, or what we call the *desmadres* drawer. This drawer is full of things that have no other place beside this drawer without order and totally without aesthetic sense. These are things of great practical and magical value like the ones you will find below.

Las Monedas: Coins

We usually throw our spare change away in the miscellaneous drawer, but coins are an indispensable magical instrument for divination and good luck.

To Make Sure You Always Have Money Where You Carry It: Wallets, handbags, and change purses are highly personal items in which we carry many things, not only our money. A lot of us carry pictures of our beloved or our kids, but many people don't realize that also we carry our own luck in these items. Many times, Mexican or not, you certainly heard your grandmother or an aunt say things like, "Do not carry your money in a wallet with holes or your money would slip out." It is incredibly important that this item is always in good condition, and that you always have money in it. Remember the famous Mexican saying, *dinero llama dinero,* "money calls money." You need something in your wallet to call more money to it.

El Volado "águila o sol?": The *volados* is the easiest, most common traditional divination method used in Mexico with which to decide luck in any aspect of life, and the one thing required is that item that any Mexican has stuck in the kitchen drawer or in our pocket: a coin. There is no Mexican who has not made an important decision in their life with the help of a coin tossed to the air (doing a volado). It can be said that this divination method is the first one we learned as kids. The famous popular phrase is, "eagle or sun?" It is very old. If you have an old Mexican coin or even one of the newest ones, you will see that on one side there is an eagle, and on the other side, most of the time, the Stone of the Sun of the Mexicas.

One thinks of the frills. It comes from the 19th century, when Mexican coins of the time had on one side the National Shield, or what we call the eagle, and on the other a Phrygian cap with sunbursts, according to the Banco de México Museum. The phrase "eagle or sun?" is so ingrained in the Mexican magical, mystical collective, within Mexican popular culture, and in our literature and cinematic art—who hasn't read *Aguila o sol* by the great Mexican poet and essayist Octavio Paz? Or watched *Heads or Tails* (Spanish: *Aguila o sol*) by Mario Moreno AKA Cantinflas's iconic film? Tossing a coin is an act of letting chance become the one who makes the decisions.

To Do a Volado: Get a Mexican coin (one, two, five, or ten pesos are recommended). Take the coin, close your hand, and blow on your fist. Open your palm and toss your coin once. While it is in the air, decide if you want to pair your question/choice with the eagle or the sun and say it out loud: aguila or sol.

In case you are doing this volado for someone else, when someone throws a coin, he must not only toss a coin. He must complete the ritual by asking a mandatory question: "eagle or sun?" and the person should decide and say it out loud. Today, the side of the coin that displays the national coat of arms is the "eagle," while the "sun" is the side that has the denomination of the piece engraved on it.

If it shows what you choose (aguila or the sol), it is then a favorable thing to go after, or a sign that an event is very, very probable.

If it is a yes or no question, the sun is always corresponds to yes and the eagle with no.

For Desperate Financial Issues: Are you faced with a desperate situation? If you have an urgent financial need, such as unexpected bills, needing extra money to pay monthly rent or mortgage payments, or if you're dealing with eviction, Saint Judas Tadeo is considered among Mexicans to be the best and fastest intercessor in financial hardships. Saint Jude was one of Jesus's twelve apostles, and his feast day is October 28. Catholic or not, a lot of us Mexicans carry the image of Saint Jude on a medal, as a scapular, or in our wallets to provide good luck and protection, and to remind us not to be afraid of the "impossible;" for nothing is impossible with Saint Jude by our side.

You will need:

- An image of St Jude (prayer stamp, statue, etc.)

- Sandalwood oil

- *Estraza* (brown craft) paper

- A pen

- Green lentils

- A gold coin (my grandma used ten pesos, you can use a dollar coin)

- Mexican clay bowl

On the estraza paper, write down the problem that you want to solve, that case that you feel is difficult to fulfill, and for which you need quick action and help. Once your petition is written, get the sandalwood oil and place some on your spirit finger (ring finger), and anoint the paper with the oil. Put the paper in the clay bowl and cover the bowl with the green lentils.

Once you have finished, place the Saint Jude image or statue on top of the bowl. If is too big, place it on the right side of your bowl. Close the petition with the following prayer:

O Holy Saint Jude, apostle and martyr, great in virtue, rich in miracles, near kinsman of Jesus Christ, faithful intercessor of all who invoke your special patronage in time of need. My Patron Saint of the Impossible, the Desperate, and the Hopeless, come to my aid, to you I have recourse from the depths of my heart and humbly beg you who God has given such great power to come assist me in this need. Help me with my present and urgent petition, bringing visible and speedy help (explain where help is almost despaired of). In return, I promise to make your name and devotion known. Saint Jude, pray for us all who invoked your aid. Amen.

When your petition is fulfilled, exchange the lentils for the coin.

La Moneda Acuñada en Año Bisiesto para la Prosperidad: It is said that if you keep a one peso coin minted in a leap year in your kitchen, it will bring good money luck to your home and family.

Los Machetes, las Tijeras, y los Cuchillos: Machetes, Scissors, and Knives

Daggers, letter openers, knives, razors, scissors, and machetes are a source of infinite magic which can be used for protection or counterattacks. In Mexican culture they can even be used for divination purposes. The following rituals are a great example of this.

Las Ligaduras

Ligatures are what a lot of people in other traditions would call sexual bindings. I talked about amarres in my book, *Mexican Sorcery*, and previously in this book as well. They are basically a marriage ceremony in the magical sense; sympathetic magic where the desired outcome is for someone to be romantically tied to another person and subjugated in different ways. With ligatures, we focus more on the sexual attraction aspect and not so much on the legal and monetary advantages that a marriage through an amarre would grant you.

Ligatures are all about romantic and sexual enchantment. The purpose is to make the target feel a sudden irresistible attraction towards someone, but this practice had other infamous and very aggressive tactics as well, like causing male impotence, paralyzing mistresses, tying someone sexually to our will, and all kind of bedroom/sexual domination benefits.

La ligadura de las tijeras

My grandma's favorite ligature was done with her magical scissors. This is by far the most iconic *ligadura* of all time in Mexico. This is a way to dominate our partner even if we are the passive one (the one receiving) in bed or in the relationship. It is said that, by doing this ligature, your sexual partner will not be able to have or even think about sex with anyone else.

You will need:

- Your magical scissors (detailed in my book, *Mexican Sorcery*)

- Three meters of red ribbon

- Your own sexual fluids

- A photo of your lover

- A nail

- A red sachet

- Red candle

- Patchouli oil

On a Friday, Venus's day, wet the three meters of red ribbon with your sexual fluids. Do not limit yourself; the more soaked it is, the better it will work. You can use your saliva, your vaginal fluid, your semen, even your sweat. Focus on that sticky, passionate, and dirty sex.

Tie three knots into this ribbon and with each knot, you will repeat the name of your lover. Take your lover's photo and wrap that ribbon around it. At the end of the knots, open your scissors and place the photograph of your lover in the middle with the ribbon between the scissors.

Light your candle and pray the following prayer:

> You will not find satisfaction until you are between my legs.
>
> Only mine, what you have between your legs will be.
>
> With no one else you will be able to find satisfaction, you will think of no one, you will remember no one, and you will satisfy no one else, as long as I put you in my fluids, ligated and tied in the knots of passion, reason, and obedience, only mine will you be.

Once you pray, leave your work in velacion all night. Place your work in the red sachet with the ribbon, rub a little patchouli on the sachet, and close your magical scissors to use in other endeavors.

To Know the Gender of a Baby

I was blessed enough to be pregnant four times in my life during a time when modern medicine in Mexico was a reality for a lot of Mexican women. My doctor used things like ultrasounds and other technological advancements to make sure my babies and I were in good health, and to know my babies' gender. That wasn't the case for my grandmother and my aunts, but they had their magical methods to know their babies' gender. I personally used this method before my doctor was able to tell me the gender of my four boys.

I have to say that our elders were very wise, even wiser than technological advancements. When I was pregnant with my third boy, the doctor told me that he was a girl, while my grandma bet it was a boy thanks to this effective method that is still used in a lot of ranches. To discover the gender of a baby, they used to place scissors and a small machete under two different chairs. If the expecting woman sat down in the chair that had the scissors, she was expecting a girl, while if she sat on the chair with the little machete, she was expecting a boy.

To confirm the gender of a baby, use the popular belly shape method, which is another traditional way to find out the sex of a baby, according to Mexican beliefs. After the seventh month, some women touch the pregnant woman's belly and divine the sex according to the shape of the belly; if the belly is pointed, it will be a girl, but if it is round it is said to be a boy.

For a Baby's Beautiful Hair
One of the most popular beliefs in Mexico is that babies' hair will grow much stronger if children are shaved during their first months of life during a waxing moon.

Carbon Vegetal
There is an element in our rural kitchens that has the capacity to absorb all impurities in the environment, even ethereal ones. This element is charcoal. It should be noted that this type of coal is not what you buy in the supermarket. That coal is contaminated with toxic chemical substances to increase its combustion. This carbon is organic and is obtained from different barks. Its powder purifies water, absorbs deleterious gases, and is used for all kinds of things. This charcoal also absorbs bad vibes and negative energies. This magical ally is mentioned in most Mexican magic books, as it is very cheap and easy to use.

You only need to place three pieces of charcoal, one by one, under the bed, at the entrance to a home, and at the entrance to your business, repeating: *In the name of the Father, the Son, and the Holy Spirit.* Leave it for three days and carefully remove the carbon in a brown paper bag.

Los Cerillos la Central: Matches

Unlike many kitchens in the United States, most Mexican kitchens have stoves that are gas and not electric. If I had to mention something that we all have in kitchens in Mexico, it would be matches. The favorite match of Mexicans is La Central brand, which is a 100 percent Mexican company that has been illuminating Mexican homes for more than 130 years, bringing matchsticks and matches of the best quality to all of Mexico, South America, and North America.

La Central match brand dates from the end of the 19th century and its current image—the one that corresponds to the line of Classic Luxury matches—is the set of iconographies of several of its products throughout history, although it is forgotten in the bottom of a drawer—and it is a success of Mexican design. If you went to visit your Mexican grandmother, I assure you that you remember this yellow box of matches with the surreal image of a Venus de Milo that seems about to be hit by a train.

To Know If Your Significant Other Is Cheating

When we have our doubts in matters of love, fire is our best ally. Fire reveals secrets, fire destroys lies, and exposes betrayals. If you think that your partner is lying to you or if you think that your significant other is being unfaithful or cheating on you, do not hesitate to do this famous ritual to find the answer you need to know.

Take three wooden matches and a piece of soap. Take a match, say your name, and stick it into the soap. Then take the next one, say the name of your significant other, and stick it in the soap as well. Finally, take the third match, say the name of the other person who you suspect your significant other is cheating with or, if you do not have a specific person in mind, simply ask if your significant other is cheating with someone else. Stick the third match in the soap. So your significant other is always in the middle, you are on the left, and the other match is on the right.

Light the three matches and you will see where the match that represents your significant other leans once the matches are burned, whether it is towards you or towards "the other one." And there you will have the answer that you need. If the match representing your significant other leans towards you, it is because he loves you and you have nothing to worry about. If that match leans towards "the other one," we can say that your significant other's soul is thinking of someone else, and you need to act soon if you want to keep your significant other or break that relationship.

To Know If Someone Is Doing Witchcraft to You

This is one of the most traditional and simple ways to know if someone is working against you magically or doing brujeria to block your blessings. If you think that you are under witchcraft or spiritual attack, perform the following ritual to confirm your suspicions.

You will need:

- A glass cup

- Holy water

- Two matches

- A prayer stamp of the Just Judge

Put the image of the Justo Juez (Just Judge) on the table or your altar. Fill the glass a little more than halfway with holy water. Place the glass on top of the stamp.

Take both matches and pass them all over your body. Once this is done, take a match and let it fall into the glass. Once that match stops moving in the water, you will add the other match.

Wait a moment for them to stop moving and there you can read the results.

If the matches are separated, it means that you are free from any witchcraft, spell, hex, ill intent, or magical work to harm you.

If the matches touch slightly, or if the matches are together and touch each other, someone tried to do witchcraft to harm you or has a shady intention against you or whoever lives in your home, and that is affecting everyone in the household.

Matches that are struck on the head means someone close to you is already doing magic or witchcraft and that evil intent is interfering with your health, well-being, workplace, luck, or romantic relationships.

Matches that touch each other's tips mean there is no brujeria, but this is an indication that you need to take necessary precautions.

Cross-shaped matches mean someone is trying to block your blessings (*cerrarte los caminos*).

Discard the water on a plant, preferably a tree, and throw the matches in the trash. Keep the stamp of the Just Judge behind the doorway of your house.

La Matatena

The *matatena* is one of the oldest and most traditional Mexican games for children and adults. The word "matatena" comes from the Nahuatl *matetema* (maitl: hand; tetl: stone; tem: fill) and means "to fill the hand with stones." This is one of the games we used to play a lot when we were children. Before, pebbles were used to play it. Today the items needed to play are a set of jacks and a small bouncing ball. The purpose of the game is to collect as many jacks as possible and then go out by playing them.

Usually sold together as a toy, the matatena has playful purposes and magical ones as well. If someone already *te lleno el buche de piedritas* (filled your insides with stones), a colloquial way Mexicans have to say that someone has already pissed us off, buy a set of matatena jacks. You can totally use your grandma's set if she allows it (the metal jacks are really good for this purpose), or you can use small pebbles. Introduce a passport photo or small picture of the person who pissed you off with the matatenas and a mixture of alcohol and thirteen habanero peppers inside of a glass jar and hide it in a dark place in your house. After some time, you will no longer feel angry. The damage done to you will have moved away and it will have returned to the one who pissed you off.

CHAPTER NINE

ANIMALS IN MEXICAN MAGIC

Domestic animals are animals that have been selected by mankind for breeding and adaptation to human environments. Over thousands of years, they have been adapting to the company of people, interacting with them in various types of contexts. The domestication process has to do with different purposes. On the one hand, there are animals who are domesticated for companionship, such as dogs and cats. On the other hand, there are animals domesticated for food, such as chickens. Finally, there is domestication for work or transportation, such as horses or donkeys.

The phrase "one eye to the cat and another to the *garabato*" arose in Mexican kitchens. The Mexican kitchens of the past were different; certain types of meat and fish had to be hung from hooks and preserved because there was no refrigerator. Over time and with the idea to prevent the food from becoming the cats' dinner, a piece of wood was installed in the middle of the kitchen or in a corner, where the sausages were hung. This was called a garabato.

"One eye to the cat and another to the garabato" is a phrase that encompasses this section, because a lot of Mexican magic is sustained on the premise of paying attention to two things at the same time without neglecting one or the other. To be completely honest, this phrase is eye-opening as to why a lot of Mexican magic was created, developed, and had its place in the kitchen. It reminded me of the most important things about Mexican magic that are getting lost to time and translations, one of which is the importance of domestic animals. Animals have been an integral part of Mexican brujas, their beliefs, and rites. Supernatural powers are even attributed to many domestic animals, as well as spiritual and magical associations with some entities, according to popular Mexican culture.

El Gato Negro

In the darkness of the night, many mysteries are kept. Over the years, some of these became popular rites and did not stay between the four walls of a kitchen or in Mexican witchcraft books. In a small town in Mexico named Mina, Nuevo León, I met a witch who mastered the black and white arts. This witch had a pet black cat. She was the one who taught me to read fortunes with fava beans. She loved old magic books, and she was the one who taught me that many Mexican magic rituals are highly influenced by ancient European and Egyptian grimoires and *ciprianillos* (the influential grimoires attributed to Saint Cyprian). A lot of these ancient grimoires suggest killing black cats on certain days, at certain hours, for things like invisibility, pacts, and trades. For the average modern Mexican bruja, this is a no-no, even for the bruja who shared this ritual with me. She was a cat lover, and her understanding of magic was at a higher level.

Modern Mexican brujas understand that magic is rarely textual or square, even less so rigid. This is what I consider to be the reason why a lot of brujas become frustrated nowadays being very literal about magical endeavors and their understanding and interpretations of ancient magic books and grimoires. See, for example, the concept of invisibility. It does not make specific reference to disappearing in the literal sense, but rather going unnoticed. In many occasions in life, it is very useful to be unnoticed to prevent negative energies, bad luck, and enemies from reaching us.

The cat, more than anything, is a representation. The cat has always been viewed as the most magical of animals, for good or for bad. For this reason, El Gato Negro was adopted as a huge source of magic in Mexico, where practicalities and laws made a lot of brujas start relying on representations and Gato Negro stamps with prayers and conjures on the back for magical purposes.

You will get a Black Cat stamp and every Tuesday at midnight, you will rub its back with a little salt, saying the following Black Cat prayer:

> ¡Oh, Planeta soberano! Tú que en ésta dominas con tu influencia a la Luna, yo te conjuro por la virtud de esta sal y de este Gato Negro en el nombre de Dios Creador, para que me concedas toda clase de bienes, tanto de salud como en tranquilidad y riquezas.

> Oh, Mighty Planet! You who dominate this with your influence, the Moon, I conjure you by virtue of this salt and this Black Cat in the name of God the Creator, so that you grant me all kinds of goods, both health and tranquility and wealth.

El Perro Prieto

A widespread belief in the ranches of Mexico was that when you had a very great need, you could have an audience with Luzbel (Lucifer). Before the rebellion he led against God, Lucifer was created beautiful, glorious, perfect. He was above all the ranks of angels and was God's favorite. Lucifer means "Bearer of Light" but when he fell, he became the Prince of Darkness.

Accessing the most beautiful star of all the fallen angels was not an easy consignment. For this one had to get a black dog that was lactating, a litter of nine black male dogs to be nursed by the bitch (in the literal sense of the word), or drink from that milk. Today, it is easier to recite the following prayer and follow the ritual below:

On a Saturday at midnight, hold a black dog's paw and recite the following prayer to dominate someone.

¡Oh, estrella encantada! ¡Oh, Luz Bella! Tú eres la más privilegiada y querida de los cielos, fuiste arrojada a la Tierra, no obstante, el gran poder que tenías en los cielos y a pesar de ser tú la más querida de Nuestro Señor, fuiste desechada porque intentaste colocar tu trono en lo más alto de lo ordenado por el Señor, y así como fuiste desechada por tu desobediencia, así yo ordeno que, con la ayuda de Lucifer, se cumpla mi mandato y con la ayuda de este perro prieto para dominar a la persona que quiero dominar (nombre de la persona a dominar).

O enchanted star! O Beautiful Light! You are the most privileged and beloved of heaven, you were thrown to Earth, however, the great power you had in heaven, and despite being the most beloved of Our Lord, you were discarded because you tried to place your throne above what was ordered by the Lord, and just as you were discarded for your disobedience, so I order that, with the help of Lucifer, my mandate be fulfilled with the help of this black dog to dominate the person I want to dominate, (name of the person to dominate).

To Make a Chronic Cheater Faithful as a Dog

Grab a pinch of *perro prieto* (black dog) hair, repeat the prayer above, and sprinkle the hair on that person's shoes.

El Caballo Negro

Ever since humankind first tamed the horse as a means of efficient transport, it has been credited with several magical attributes including power, vigor, and swiftness. *El caballo negro* is a powerful dark invocation to different entities, including Lucifer. However, the caballo negro should always be controlled by the rider (the bruja). This powerful invocation steed is headstrong.

> *Alma del caballo negro, anima de Juan el minero, alma de Lucifer; y su mensajero el charro negro que por aquellas barrancas que subiste y bajaste, por las veredas cabalgaste y sin cansar galopaste tráeme de regreso el amor de mi vida a pies humillado, arrepentido, y desesperado.*

> Soul of the black horse, soul of Juan the miner, soul of Lucifer, and his messenger, the black charro, through those ravines that you climbed and descended, along the paths you rode, and without tiring you galloped, bring back the love of my life to my feet, humiliated, repentant, and desperate.

La Gallina Negra

The most accepted version of the arrival of hens suggests that Spanish and Portuguese colonizers introduced chickens when they arrived on the eastern shores of America, even though the beginning of the use of black hens in Mexican magical history is still widely unknown. Evidence suggests that

European occult and supernatural books such as *La Gallina Negra* (*La Poule Noire*) and *El Libro de San Cipriano,* among others, are where this powerful being originated. The black hen is a symbol of cleansing and protection in Mexican witchcraft. The black hen is used for heavy cleansings. It protects you and frees you from envy, the evil eye, and enemies. The black hen's egg is used to cleanse, especially when there is suspicion of an evil eye or that a person is suffering from a malediction.

> *Dios y señor nuestro que esta gallina negra, tu divina creación despoje de todo mal, mal de ojo, maldición, conjuro maléfico, hechos con o sin mala intención y que ese daño y maldad se materialice a través de este huevo/veladora para que pueda verlo, y regresarlo a donde pertenece.*

> God and our Lord, will that this black hen, your divine creation, strip of all evil, evil eye, curse, malefic spell, made with or without bad intentions, and that this damage and evil materialize through this egg/candle so that it can see it and put it back where it belongs.

The Huitzilin/El Colibrí

The art crafting of love amulets in Mexican magic is one of the most iconic practices that dates back to pre-Hispanic times. This is one that I consider the most important, which inspired and developed other magical goods, inspired by the original version, like prayers, candles, oils, perfumes, powders, and crafted baths, as well as others. The hummingbird depicts the Aztec God Huitzilopochtli (the Hummingbird), who was conceived by his mother after she clutched a ball of hummingbird feathers to her breasts. In Mexico, the hummingbird is known as the love bird. The following information is meant to clarify and give some historical and ritualistic context about this belief and not to recreate or contribute to the hummingbird black market in Mexico.

The use of the hummingbird in magical endeavors dates back to pre-Hispanic times, and, after the colonization, the use of the hummingbird as an amulet was common among the whole population. The Inquisition records suggest that this amulet was used among every social class and every caste and was equally carried by males and females. The natives were the ones controlling the monopoly of the production, crafting, and distribution of this magical love amulet. Even today, in a lot of places in Mexico, such as mercados and botanicas, there is a black market for this precious bird.

Today it is very common to find hummingbird inspired products, usually in the *chuparosa* (the female bird) modality. I was able to find only one mercado with *chupamirto* (the male bird), and there were not a lot of these products. I find that it's really difficult, almost impossible, to find the chupamirto crafts here in the US. Luckily, you can use chuparosa in the place of both since it is pretty gender neutral. It is worth mentioning that hummingbirds of whatever gender are attracted equally to the nectar of myrtle or rose plants, but the name is given colloquially since the myrtle flower is tubular and elongated (very similar to the penis in its shape and size); likewise, the rose resembles a vagina.

You absolutely do not need to harm a bird for this amulet to attract a lover. You only need follow this proven recipe.

The first thing you need to do is understand the nature of the hummingbird. It doesn't matter if is a chuparosa or a chupamirto; how do you attract one? Hummingbirds differ from other birds in that their principal food source is nectar. They are naturally attracted to the color red, which is why most nectar feeders you see have a red base or top. The *morralitos* (charm bags for amulets) are red as well. A lot of Mexican abuelas in general are bird lovers. My Grandma Socorro, for example, used to have *mirto* planted in her garden, and she would hang red ribbons on feeders and the branches of her trees, because hummingbirds are attracted to red colors. The same color reminds them of the flowers that supply their sweet nectar and activate their appetite. Red blossoms are associated with the heart, which is an important Aztec symbol that still to this day represents and calls for passion, love, and lust.

Chuparosa/Chupamirto Ritual

To attract a romantic partner into your life, follow the same method that you would follow to attract a hummingbird to your backyard, while incorporating a magical and powerful Mexican traditional prayer.

You will need:

- A chuparosa or chupamirto charm

- A chuparosa or red candle

- Sugar

- Water

- A small glass jar (you can use a baby food container)

- Red ribbon

- Mirto (*Salvia microphylla*) red tubular flower (if you can't find mirto in your area, you can use dried red rose petals)

- Ven a Mi oil

On a Friday, gather all the materials together. Craft the nectar by bringing two cups of water to a boil. Add half a cup of white granulated sugar, preferably organic. Stir with intention until the sugar is dissolved, focusing on the kind of lover you would like to attract to your life, and then allow this mix to thoroughly cool.

Once you have your mix, put the nectar in the small jar after adding the chuparosa charm.

Once you have decanted it, wash your hands with the rest of the nectar and proceed to do a velacion. Dress the candle with the oil and the dried mirto flowers or red rose petals. Wash your hands again to remove any stickiness. Light your candle and place it close to the jar until the candle is finished. Once the candle is finished, open the jar and take out the charm. Place it on the red ribbon that you will use as a bracelet.

Rub the bracelet with the Ven a Mi oil while you pray the following prayer:

> Oh, divine Chuparosa/Chupamirto, you who give and take away the nectar of the flowers, you who give life and instill love, I welcome you and your powerful fluids. Protect me and make me lovable to as many (men/women or mention the name of a specific target) as I want. Well, I swear to you by all the spirits of the Holy Apostles not to stop for a moment from adoring you in your sacrosanct reliquary so that you grant me what I ask of you, my beautiful friend. I invoke your great power to have my beloved attracted to me, submissive and humble, eating from my hand.
>
> Amen.

Tie three knots and with each knot pray a Hail Mary.

Chuparosa/Chupamirto
Amulet to Attract a Lover

This amulet, known for its natural compositions and perfect combinations of its elements, has been one of the most popular since time immemorial. The mixture of different components has traditionally been used by men and women who seek the arrival of love in their lives.

For this amulet, you will need:

- A red morralito

- A red string

- White rice

- Cotton
  (preferably cotton nesting material)

- A chuparosa charm

- A chunk of piloncillo

- Red roses oil

- Copal incense

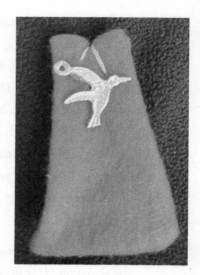

Moisten the rice and the cotton with the oil and introduce it into the red morralito, along with a piece of paper bearing the name of the person you would like to attract or, in case you do not have someone specific in mind, with the characteristics of the type of person that you would like to attract into your life. After you have it ready, light your copal incense and pass the morralito through the smoke nine times, and then add the chunk of piloncillo and repeat:

> Oh, divine Chuparosa, you who gives and takes the nectar
> from the flowers, give me my lover and take away this loneliness
> from my life.

Introduce the chuparosa charm to the morralito and tie the morralito bag closed. Tie three knots. Pray the sign of the cross three times, one for each knot, before burning the loose ends of the cords with a match. (Be careful not to burn the bag or yourself.) Afterwards, spray the bag with a little of your perfume or cologne. Carry it with you, always hidden and pinned on your left side.

Against Poisonous Animals

Poisonous animals are all those that have a gland that produces venom and the ability to inject it into another living being. There is a huge variety of poisonous animals in Mexico, and they are a threat to everyone, both people and pets. The best known, especially in our country, are spiders and scorpions, forms that other witches usually take through rituals or creatures that are sent as curses or spells. One of the best defenses against poisonous animals, other witches taking these forms, or curses sent through an animal's venom is this ancient and powerful prayer, which is made in conjunction with a ritual. (If you are bitten or stung by a venomous animal, please seek medical attention immediately.)

On a Tuesday, tie a red cord on your pinky before reciting the following prayer.

San Jorge Bendito, amarra tus animalitos con un cordoncito bendito para que no nos piquen ni los grandes ni los chiquitos.

Saint George Blessed, tie your little animals with a blessed cord so that neither the big nor the little ones sting us.

CHAPTER TEN

CULTURAL ISSUES AND SOLUTIONS

Magic in the Bedroom: Enchanting the Love Enclosure

There was a custom in colonial times, and especially during the Second French Intervention in Mexico, that, with time, became a tradition. This custom called for enchanting and doing something special with the space where a sexual encounter was going to take place. Who doesn't remember that famous scene in Laura Esquivel's novel *Like Water for Chocolate*, when Tita suffered temporary blindness due to the whiteness of the matrimonial sheet that Gertrudis and Chencha were embroidering for Rosaura's wedding night?

Many of our elders had the great task of not only purifying but enchanting these bedrooms. All these formulas were different; the same ones couldn't be used for a wedding night as for a room in a brothel. These practices have been forgotten because today we focus more and more on material and financial issues. The health benefits of sex go beyond the physical; it also impacts our self-esteem and the hormones that influence happiness. Sex, intimacy, and pleasure are important, and if we can have magical help that allows us not only to attract but also to improve our performance in bed, this will significantly influence our lives.

This procedure is carried out before the person with whom the sexual encounter will take place arrives. Make sure that the room is clean and tidy. Clean sheets and a ventilated place are a must. This formula is specially composed to attract that special person to your bed. In addition, it will help make sure that this person will return to your bed, begging for more.

Talcum powder has been used for all kinds of cleaning and beauty-related purposes for years. Talcum powder is often associated with babies, but it has endless uses in Mexican witchcraft. Talcum is a mineral made up of magnesium, silica, oxygen, and hydrogen. The extracted mineral is processed, purified, and mixed with perfumes and other substances for the skin. Maja brand perfumed talcum powder has been used since 1918 in such a way that it manages to make anyone fall in love with its fragrance. The unmistakable, timeless, and characteristic aroma of Maja has managed to transcend generation after generation, becoming a classic with different uses. This old formula also has the virtue of capturing or attracting the affection of the person you love, or recovering a loved one when the main objective is to ignite the flame of passion again.

To make this formula, mix clean nail filings from your own nails and Maja talc. These are the only components of this formula. The talc container is made of plastic, so you can easily store it in the bathroom or carry it without any problem in your purse if you know that this encounter will take place at a hotel. You only need to spread a little on the bed where you are going to have the sexual encounter.

In case you do not have access to Maja talc, you can make your own formula with easily accessible ingredients.

You will need:

- 50 grams of cornstarch

- 50 grams of rice flour

- 50 grams of baking soda

- Crushed dried rose petals and lavender

- Ten drops of rose essential oil and two drops of Ven a Mi oil

- Nail filings (yours)

In a glass container with a large lid, mix the cornstarch, rice flour, baking soda, your nail filings, and the crushed dried rose petals and lavender. Add the rose essential oil and then Ven a Mi oil and mix again. Let it rest for forty-eight hours and then mix it again. Sift it to remove the bits of dried flowers and then put it in a *talquera* (talc container).

For an extra kick, it is recommended that you put the mix (either the one already made with Maja or the one made from scratch) in velacion on a Friday, using either a red candle or a Ven a Mi seven day candle.

Caution: A lot of our grandmothers and mothers had the habit of using talc in their intimate areas. Never use these mixtures on the genital area, as it is associated with an increased risk of ovarian cancer. In fact, talc is no longer used as a dry lubricant for surgical gloves because it is believed to become toxic when applied to mucosal tissue.

Las Pisadas: Footsteps

Footsteps are known as one of the most successful, ancient works that guarantee quick results. People who use this type of trick are those who want to control the steps of and subdue a person or control them against their will to obtain some benefit. This age-old trick is considered a work of domination.

If you want to bring someone back and dominate and control this person's everything, you are going to need this from your target: a shoe. In case you can't get access to their shoes, you can use the dirt or dust the target has stepped in. Even if the footprint is pretty much invisible, you can pretend to "clean" the floor where this person stood with a kitchen towel or a napkin in order to trap the footprint there. That same napkin is going to be the one you use for this domination working. Once you have the shoe or footprint, bury the dirt, napkin, or shoe in a pot inside of your house, with the heel always facing towards your bedroom. Be creative!

Safety Pin and Red Ribbon

Eclipses during pregnancy have been one of the biggest concerns for many Mexican women for generations. The Aztecs believed that eclipses could cause harm to the unborn baby. They thought that eclipses happened because the sun bit the moon, or vice versa, and if a pregnant woman was exposed to this phenomenon, her child might be born with some malformation or defect. This myth was modified, and it was then thought that eclipses could cause cleft lip in babies.

It is believed that if the woman is exposed to a solar eclipse, the baby can be born blind, so most Mexican moms use a safety pin pinned in their underwear for protection. Thanks to eclipses, many myths have arisen, but also so have protections. The best known is that the pregnant women should wear a red ribbon and a safety pin.

San Gerardo de Mayella Bracelet

Saint Gerard Majella is the patron saint of expectant mothers, mothers, women in childbirth, and unborn children. In Mexico he is known as "the saint of pregnancies that can be carried to term." A very common practice is, when learning that a woman is pregnant, she is given a bracelet with the image of San Gerardo to protect both the mother and the child throughout the pregnancy so that through the protection of this benevolent saint a healthy baby is born.

You can buy or craft your own bracelet as well as soon as you know that you are pregnant. This is especially important if you have suffered several miscarriages or high-risk pregnancies. Wear a bracelet of pink and baby blue beads with the Saint Medal and do not take it off until after the forty days of postpartum confinement. It is said that in some ranchos our grandmothers used to bury the bracelet along with the placenta after childbirth.

A prayer card and bracelet for San Gerardo de Mayella.

Evil Eye in Babies

The evil eye causes a lot of discomfort and different symptoms in babies. In general, these symptoms appear after the baby or infant has been in contact with someone who is considered heavy-eyed or has looked at them with exaggerated admiration. (This is common with beautiful babies, babies with big eyes, or when parents dress them in clothes that are too showy.) This can occur intentionally or unintentionally. The heavy eyes are believed to heat up the child's blood. The most common symptoms of the evil eye in babies are the following: uncontrollable crying, crankiness, hot temperature for no apparent reason, altered sleep pattern, loss of appetite, and in some cases vomiting, among other symptoms.

Mal de ojo (the evil eye) is the most reported folk illness among Mexican and Latino families in the United States. That is why Mexican mothers and especially grandmothers generally look for popular magical methods to protect their babies from the evil eye, as a way of prevention, as well as other methods to cure babies of the evil eye.

The first thing that you should do when you detect either yourself or another person possibly giving the evil eye to a baby (again we can give evil eye by admiring a baby), is what every seasoned abuela will say/do to avoid mal de ojo which is . . . *tocalo por que le haces ojo!* To counteract the effects of the evil eye, the admirer should touch the baby. I know this can be difficult, culturally speaking.

The second method is gifting the baby with a charm or amulet on a necklace or bracelet to provide protection against the evil eye. These protections are commonly used by adults as well. Among them are:

Ojo de Venado: Eye of a Deer: This traditional Mexican amulet has been used for centuries. The "eye of the deer" refers not to an actual deer's eye but to the dark brown seed of *mucuna pruriens,* the velvet bean. These seeds are commonly made into bracelets. These bracelets are usually made during the spring when there is abundant supply of seeds. The amulet itself represents an eye. It is strung on a red cord and finished off with a plump red wool tassel, with a Catholic Saint image imprinted on it. The saint is usually La Virgen de Guadalupe, el Santo Nino de Atocha, or Saint Jude. This cord is traditionally placed around the baby/infant's left wrist as a bracelet.

Azabache Bracelets: The *azabache* jet bracelet is a powerful protection amulet against the evil eye that has been used for a long time. To counteract the evil eye, it must be worn on the left hand.

Pulsera Roja: Less is more and that is why I consider that the red bracelet is the simplest, most powerful, and safest amulet against the evil eye and danger to babies and infants. It is as simple as tying a bracelet on the baby's left wrist. Use red ribbon or thread previously blessed with holy water, taking care that this bracelet fits the baby comfortably and not tightly so as not to hurt them.

Mexican culture has its own version of the evil eye folklore, and it is believed that the color red has the virtue of warding off and fighting the evil eye, in addition to providing protection. Red is thought to divert the admirer's attention away from the baby or infant.

Medallas de Santos: Many parents used to give babies a guardian angel *medallita*, or a medal of the Virgin of Guadalupe or another saint to keep them protected, since many of them can be petitioned for protection against the evil eye. Among the most common medals are the Archangel Gabriel, who is the protector of pregnant mothers and newborns, and Saint Benedict of Nursia to protect the baby from evil spirits and entities.

Family Protection: One of the traditions in Mexican culture when it comes to putting these bracelets on a baby is for someone in the family to give it to the child. It is said that this gives the amulet more strength, because it is given with love and in good faith.

A safe and smart alternative is to pin the azabache or the ojo de venado on the inside of a garment or place the bracelet on the left foot of the baby or infant.

To Cure Mal de Ojo in a Baby

Popular tradition suggests that there are several ways to cure the evil eye in babies, ranging from the most common, such as *una limpia con huevo* (egg cleansing), to others such as prayers and magical *ensalmos* (folk healings), which must always be performed after blessing ourselves with the sign of the cross. The following prayers and ensalmos have been passed down from generation to generation because they are an effective and efficient way to cure and alleviate the evil eye.

Limpia con Huevo

An egg is a cleansing agent like no other. An egg has healing properties and possesses the virtue of absorbing and removing spiritual diseases such as the evil eye. Since ancient times, our parents and grandparents used an egg cleanse as a ritual to restore health in both babies and adults. The ritual is very simple and can be performed for more than just curing the evil eye.

You will need:

- A chicken egg (the color of the shell does not matter)

- A glass of holy water (the glass must be made of glass and completely transparent)

To cleanse a baby, you must first have faith that this will help to cure the evil eye. Be certain that we have spiritual help and that we can heal through and with the help of the divine power of our creator. It is recommended that the person who performs this ritual first bless themselves and then pray an Our Father to ask for spiritual help. Second, the baby or infant must be in a comfortable position. They can be lying on their bed or sitting, and they must also wear light clothing, such as cotton. Do not dress the baby in layers such as a sweater or a jacket. Third, make sure you have everything you need before you get started, so you can perform your *limpia* (cleansing) without interruptions.

Grab the egg with your dominant hand. The egg must be at room temperature. Slowly move the egg while praying the Apostles' Creed all the way down the baby's body, starting at their head and ending in their feet in this order:

- baby's fontanelle

- right temple

- left temple

- right ear

- left ear

- nape

- top of the head and neck

- head (a cross is made with the egg along the head)

- heart

- chest

- right arm and hand

- left arm and hand

- right shoulder

- left shoulder

- back (a cross is made across the length and width of the back)

- from left to right at the waist

- stomach and belly

- right thigh knee

- left thigh knee

- diaper front and diaper behind (always in the presence and with permission of the parents)

- right armpit

- left armpit

- a cross is made along the entire body (from head to toes)

You must repeat this operation three times. Trust your intuition. If you feel called to stay in a particular area of the baby's body for a bit longer or to rub the egg for longer in an area, do that.

Pray the Apostle's Creed.

Now crack the egg into the glass of water, then flush the entire contents of the glass down the toilet, depending on how good your plumbing is. Most people in Mexico discard the shells in the trash can.

The Mexican Suegras for Your Monster-in-Law

Yes, you read it right! Monster-in-law! That's what a lot of *suegras* (mother-in-laws) are for many of us in Mexico. Some few become a second mother, the mother we did not have, or that we wished to have, and are truly a blessing. In Mexico, the word "suegra" is used to refer to the mother of your significant other, even if you're not married but rather in a relationship that is more serious.

In Mexico, mothers-in-laws are a big part of one's family, and a lot of times they become noisy, controlling, and a real headache for a couple. There are different types of suegras. The machista ones, the dramatic ones, the manipulative ones, the critical ones, I could go on and on and on. The truth is that a lot of marriages and good relationships have dissolved due their toxicity. I bet, if you are Latino, you understand these toxic dynamics or have heard these stories. Your own mom probably dealt with this. It is important to note that the responsibility for setting limits should be with your partner, because if they continue to allow these behaviors, things will continue to happen. On your part, you need a lot of strength to set clear limits, and when these are crossed not to break and end up giving in for love, which many Mexican women end up doing because that is what has been instilled in us since we were little.

This is a very old and effective trabajo. If you can't get her to love you (some mothers-in-law are very hard-headed), at least this will make her "sweeten" her attitude towards you. You will need:

- Estraza paper

- A pen

- A picture of your suegra (you can do this for your *suegro*, your father-in-law, as well in case he is the toxic one. If they are both toxic, you can use a picture of them together.)

- A small glass jar

- Honey

- A Mexican clay plate

- A baby blue candle

- A dark *paliacate* (a rag or bandana)

Take the photograph and write the name or names of your in-laws.

Then take your pen and paper and write the following: *From now on (your mother-in-law's name), you stop being . . .* and then you name the toxic and negative attitudes that you want to eliminate from your mother-in-law (hatred, criticism, meddling, gossip, to name a few). Roll the paper into a scroll and insert the photograph and the paper into the jar.

After placing the paper and photograph in the jar, coat the paper with honey and totally fill the jar with it. Close the jar. Put the jar in velacion (very close to candlelight) until the candle is consumed. Wrap the jar in the paliacate. Bury the jar on your patio or in a pot with a flower on top of it, so your significant others or your kids never find that trabajo.

The aim of this trabajo is to keep a relationship with your in-laws and make it more pleasant. In case that isn't your goal, you have several other options in this book.

Infidelity in Mexican Culture

One of the biggest challenges in Mexican culture when it comes to being married is infidelity. There are several reasons for this, but one of them is cultural. We are immersed in a sexist culture and infidelity is part of being macho, or it is viewed as a challenge for men, even when the man in question is married or in an established relationship. Do not get me wrong: women can cheat as well, but in our culture, both traditionally and today, the woman is subject to public scrutiny. In Mexico, female infidelity is viewed socially as worse than male infidelity. The most surprising thing is that this perception is shared in many cases by Mexican women themselves.

In theory, monogamous marriage is the basis of the Mexican constitution and society. In practice, this is not usually the case. These are some of the tips and recipes from aunts and grandmothers to prevent or stop this infidelity, depending on what you need.

To Keep a Sancho or Sancha Away

Sancho/sancha is a slang word used for a sidepiece, as in a spouse or girlfriend who is being unfaithful with a sancho. Sancha is the feminine equivalent. If you already know who this sancho or sancha is and where this person lives, you will need:

- Three eggs (the larger the better)

- A black candle

- Cemetery dirt

- A bowl

- A pair of gloves

Once you have both gloves on your hands, place the eggs in the bowl and cover them with the cemetery dirt. (It's important to wear gloves when handling cemetery dirt.) Light the black candle and draw a cross on top of that dirt with the melted wax, focusing on the sancho or sancha. Leave the trabajo marinating for three days, then take the eggs out of the bowl and place them in a safe place in order to transport them to the target's house. Break the eggs in front of the target's home with all your hatred while focusing on this person's fear for their wellbeing and that they quit the relationship they have with your loved one.

For Baby's Hiccups

Hiccups do not normally harm a baby, but they make our baby uncomfortable. There is a magical popular belief among Mexican families about a home remedy to eliminate baby hiccups. This consists of wetting a red thread with saliva that must be placed on the baby's forehead. It is a remedy that has been created thanks to Mexican grannies. Another remedy to make hiccups disappear is to give the child a slight fright or a surprise, but this is only suitable for older children.

To Capture a Criminal and Do Justice

Juan is not a brujo, and he did not always believe in magic. Rather, he was a smart young man with a lot of belief in science and one of my brothers' best friends. Juan decided to study criminology. In Mexico, this profession is a social science and is the study of the causes and circumstances of the different crimes, the personality of criminals, and the appropriate treatment. He got to know many people, some alive and many others dead. He treated both with the same respect.

As a criminologist, Juan's job consisted of seeking to prevent crime and capturing those responsible for it, but in a country like Mexico, this is not always possible. In Mexico, injustice goes hand in hand with corruption, and after a few years, Juan was about to resign and look for another career until a veteran criminologist who was about to retire shared something that changed his mind. He shared the same with me one afternoon.

When someone is murdered, three knots should be tied in their shirt so that the murderer does not escape and is promptly apprehended. If this cannot be done because the dead person is not wearing a shirt (a common case with raped women), it is also customary to tie the big toes of the person's feet with a black ribbon, making the three knots in the ribbon to ensure that the criminal will not escape. The man who shared this told Juan that it was a common practice in rural areas where people did not have police and criminologists as they do in big cities. What Juan mentioned is that it is very effective, and that it totally changed his magical and spiritual views and opinions.

Against Brujas and Brujeria: Inside Out Underwear

To scare away evil spirits and witches, clothes, such as underwear, should be worn inside out. Wearing inside out underwear is without a doubt the oldest shield of protection to repel all evil.

Lemons Against Witchcraft

If you hear strange sounds in your house, see shadows, or you feel bad energy in the environment, such as heaviness, discouragement, and fear ... all these are signs that something is beginning to affect your spiritual environment and that you must remove it quickly and effectively. Our abuelas used this easy, effective, and successful method once they started to feel something was not quite right. This must be done the following Friday after you realize something is wrong, at 3:00 p.m.

Cut three lemons crosswise and put them in clean water for seven hours, in addition to praying three Creeds. Use this water to wash your hands and clean the door of your house.

To Untie the Knots of Your Life

In the middle of the jungle in southern Mexico is the Sanctuary of Our Lady, Undoer of Knots, in Cancun, Quintana Roo. You can see more than half a million ribbons hanging in her atrium. These ribbons represent problems that people have not been able to solve and for which they need a miracle.

Visitors hang these ribbons as reminders to the Virgin Mary to intercede for them in all kinds of problems, but especially those related to health, love, and financial problems. Through this practice, the faithful ask for the intercession of the Virgin Mary so that she "unties the knots" that complicate their life. The last time I visited Cancun with my family, I had the opportunity to visit this beautiful sanctuary, but if you do not have a way to visit Mexico right now, you can untie the knots of your life by doing this ritual.

One Monday, take forty centimeters of white ribbon. Tie nine knots in the ribbon and pray the miraculous prayer written below to the Virgin. Each night before you go to bed, untie one of the nine knots. When you finish the nine days and have untied the nine knots, a white candle should be offered to Maria la Desatanudos.

> *Holy Blessed Mother, you who are full of grace today I ask you to release the knots and ties that arise in my life.*
>
> *Untie the knots that prevent me from leading a peaceful life, untie the knots so I can achieve my peace and spiritual harmony. Untie, Blessed Mother, the knots that prevent me from being, fully living my days with happiness and joy.*
>
> *Untie the knots of my fears, doubts, debts, anxiety, uncertainty, sadness, and everything that does not let me advance in my life.*
>
> *Untie the knots of my heart, so I can trust my being to your maternal care.*
>
> *Amen.*

Do it with a lot of faith and a lot of strength so that your request is heard and fulfilled.

CHAPTER ELEVEN

MEXICAN CHRISTMAS AND MAGIC FOR THE NEW YEAR

Guadalupe Reyes Marathon

The December holidays are times of so much magic. Traditionally, a lot of abuelitas' magic happens during this time of the year, which means that it is the perfect time to perform the best rituals and attract prosperity and abundance to our home and our lives. The Guadalupe Reyes Marathon is considered by Mexicans to be the longest festival of the year, starting on December 12, Guadalupe's Day, and ending January 6, Three Kings' Day.

This season, which is born from popular culture, encompasses all the holidays that are celebrated in Mexico in December and early January.

Guadalupe's Offerings

Religion has made us believe that Guadalupe's temple is in Mexico, in the Tepeyac. But we know that her temple is actually in our grandmas' house, in their kitchens and their hands, every time they put them together to pray for us, and then use those same bare hands to clean *frijoles* and to roast the maize, to make tamales and transform the gifts of *tonantzin*, (a Nahuatl word composed of to [our] + nān [mother] + tzin [honorific tittle] meaning our sacred mother of sustenance), into sustenance, into our daily bread. That's where her temple is: in their kitchens, in our hearts. When I was not able to travel to Mexico due to my immigration status, I consoled myself by thinking and doing the things that I share today with you. The Virgin of Guadalupe is an important religious symbol, but at the same time she is a symbol of national identity for Mexicans. Her faith transcends borders, since she is also recognized as the Patroness of the Americas.

December 12 is a very important day for us in Mexico, since it is celebrated as the Virgin of Guadalupe's feast. She is our mom, our protector. She is very important to us, and we love her and honor her. To open a magical Guadalupe Reyes, light a Guadalupe prayer candle in her honor and ask her for blessings and protection for yourself and your beloved family members. If you, like me, are the foody type, you can offer her a meal made with your hands, one that includes maize.

Las Posadas: December 16th to the 24th

The word *posada* means inn or lodging. Traditionally there are nine posadas. These parties celebrate the journey that Jose and Maria (Joseph and Mary) took to reach Belen. Traditional posadas feature pinatas, *buñuelos*, and awesome *ponches de frutas* (fruit punch).

Mexican Christmas

It's not about the date, it's about the memories. It is not about the religious meaning, it is about the gathering, the food, the flavors, and the traditional Mexican decorations. Mexican Christmas is full of magical meaning like no other celebration. December 24 is Christmas Eve, when the family traditionally reunites to have dinner and celebrate together. Although in Mexico the day we refer as Christmas is actually Christmas Eve, a lot of families reunite again to have another Christmas gathering on the twenty-fifth. There are a lot of elements that are very traditional and somehow magical. One of the things you can incorporate into your practice during Christmas is Mexican Christmas inspired decor.

According to Mexican scholars and academics, the emperor Maximilian of Habsburg and his wife Carlota brought the first Christmas tree to Mexico. Common people implemented this tradition of decorating a Christmas tree in Mexican homes after 1878, when General Miguel Negrete placed one in his own house. The best things you can add to a Christmas tree are ornaments that reflect your culture, your beliefs, the lives of your ancestors, your family journey, and those things that already make your own family tree shine brightly and beautifully.

To decorate your home and your tree and have a magical season, consider the following.

Noche Buenas Flowers

The *cuetlaxóchitl,* as it is known, is characterized by having the appearance of a vibrant red star. Its meaning in Nahuatl is "flower that withers." It was planted in the gardens of the Aztec rulers and used as an offering in religious ceremonies. It was considered a symbol of purity and it also had medicinal and ornamental uses. The best place to put your *noche buenas* is where it is visible to the outside, as this will make all the positive vibes enter your house and protect your household. Place your noche buenas at the entrance of the house, on a balcony, or even on your Christmas tree. You can use synthetic ones. A lot of us place them in an odd number so that your home is always full of peace and harmony.

Rosemary

After the noche buenas, rosemary is one of the most important herbs in Mexico during Christmas. Although it does not give off the typical pine smell, it does give off an aroma that reminds us of Mexican Christmas. In addition, we take advantage of this time of the year and add some rosemary sachets for protection, abundance, and prosperity. Rosemary is linked to María and baby Jesus.

Seven Coins

Seven coins under the tree: the origins of this tradition are not clear, but it establishes that seven coins must be placed under the Christmas tree to take care of the home economy. Preferably they are put in the manger under the tree for better results.

Tiny Piñatas

There are two versions of the origin of piñatas. The first dates to ancient China. The other version is attributed to Mayan civilization, since it is said that they played a game blindfolded. This game consisted of hanging a clay pot full of cocoa beans with a rope and trying to break it. After the conquest, piñatas became a resource for evangelization. It was in that period when the piñata was given the shape of a star with seven peaks, which represented the seven deadly sins, although in some states of Mexico it is much more common to see these donkey-shaped piñatas because they are said to be the figure that the devil used to disguise himself in the mangers.

The truth is that it is a tradition that is deeply rooted in Mexican culture. It has many very mystical elements and can even be said to be esoteric, full of messages for those who are open to receiving them.

When the piñata is hung, it is customary to sing while a person tries to break it. Piñatas are generally adorned with brightly colored stripes and ruffles. These symbolize the temptations of life, vanity, and the mundane aspects in our lives. The stick that is used to hit the piñata and break it simulates the force with which evil, falsehood, and deceit are destroyed. The fruits and sweets that are usually placed inside the piñata symbolize the blessings received through faith. The blindfold symbolizes your faith even in uncertainty.

Hang a Key to Open Your Paths

There is only one thing that scares us Mexicans more than *el cucuy* (the Mexican bogeyman) and La Llorona (a macabre story about a female ghost who drowned her children) and that is the January slope. The January slope is associated with the end of the holidays and the excesses that come with them, but in reality, it occurs due to two main factors. On the one hand, the adjustment of prices on some products and services, in addition to the payment of property taxes, car taxes, as well as credit cards that are sometimes saturated with holiday purchases. To help you face the *cuesta de enero*, hang a key on your tree to open your paths to new opportunities and extra money.

A Donkey

El burro is one of the main Christmas characters in Mexico. There is a lot of folklore surrounding this animal. The legend tells us that the donkey that carried Jesus into Jerusalem on Palm Sunday followed him to Calvary. Appalled by the sight of Jesus on the cross, the donkey turned away but could not leave. It is said that the shadow of the cross fell upon the shoulders and back of the donkey. The cross marking found on many donkeys today remains as a testimony of the love and devotion of the donkey. In many parts of Mexico, it is said that the donkey is the devil disguised to be able to get closer to the manger. Each traditional figure in a *Nacimiento* (the birth of Jesus) is symbolic of something. The donkey is one of my favorite figures in the Nacimiento. He represents the strongest animal in all creation, chosen to carry Mary. In theory, there are stronger animals than a donkey, but the donkey teaches us that physical strength is nothing compared to the strength of our spirit and our will.

A Star at the Top of Your Tree

Whose abuelita didn't have a star on her tree or her Nacimiento? The Star of Bethlehem reminds us that the birth of Jesus wasn't announced to everyone, even though the star was shining bright on the sky. Accordingly, in Mexican folklore, the highest authorities, the Sanhedrin, the *escribas,* were not there at the manger. They were not called to be at the manger, not because they were ignorant but because they were not wise. Only the spirit filled ones, the Three Wise Men, the shepherds, the outsiders, and even the devil himself were present.

December 28: El Dia de los Inocentes

The 28th of December, Innocent's Day, is the day of jokes. It is the equivalent of April Fool's Day. Do never lend money on this day because you are never going to be paid back.

December 31st: Noche Vieja

The last night of the year is known as *noche vieja* (New Year's Eve), and usually families gather around the table to talk about the good, the bad, and the ugly of that year. To celebrate, there is a late party with a lot of good food and a lot of drinks. Here is some magical advice that you should never forget to follow.

La Barrida de Año Nuevo: New Year's Sweeping

Attracting good fortune and getting rid of bad vibes are goals that we pursue in many New Year's rituals. A deeply rooted Mexican custom to receive the new year is to clean the house thoroughly just before the end of the year. It is especially important to sweep towards the door to eliminate negativity and bad energy that left the old year.

Año Nuevo, Zapatos Nuevos: New Year, New Shoes

Shoes are like friends; they can hold you up or bring you down. We owe much of our comfortable life to our shoes. A good pair of shoes is underrated most of the time and it's up to us to realize that they are an essential part of our wardrobe. My grandmother was a very observant bruja who used to check every single and minimal detail, but the first thing she looked at was someone's shoes. She used to tell her clients, *Nuevo año sólo se le conquista con la suela de nuestros zapatos.* (The new year, all can only be conquered with the sole of our shoes.) There are a lot of shoe rituals and magic mixed with our Mexican traditions.

This shoe ritual is super famous in northern Mexico. The ritual consists of buying new shoes to use on December 31, if you can. If not, you can clean your existing shoes very thoroughly. After rubbing the new or clean sole with abre caminos oil, introduce a coin or a bill inside of the left shoe while praying the following prayer to open your roads.

> *In the name of my Almighty God, may this powerful oil open the Paths where I will walk to (here say the year). Let the roads open for me both on a personal level and as a professional; that is the virtue of this abre caminos oil. Take away all wickedness, stumbles that I may have in my walk; that for every road that I walk the*

steps are for my benefit and that in (mention the year) there will be
no obstacle that closes the roads for me. May my paths be open and
may they appear free, clean, clear, unlocked.

Amen.

El Cubetazo de Agua: The Water Bucket

One of the most popular traditions in Mexico is throwing water out the
window. This tradition is better known as *el cubetazo* and consists of throwing a bucket of water into the street. It is said that this tradition drives away
the sorrows of the past year and thus welcomes one full of prosperity and
happiness.

El Frasco de la Abundancia para Año Nuevo: New Year's Abundance Jar

The belief in the spiritual and magical power of seeds dates back thousands
of years. In Mexico, seeds are one of the most important and basic foods
in our households, so having them at home is a symbol of prosperity. It is
believed that having them prevents a lack of what is necessary at home. The
abundance jar is one of the effective New Year's rituals to attract prosperity
and abundance. It is one of the most popular because the materials used
to prepare it are very easy to find, and a lot of times we already have them
in our pantry. This jar is made during the month of December before New
Year's. Once it is made, you put it behind your entry door to receive the new
year. After that, it can be part of your kitchen decoration the rest of the year.

You will need:

- A glass jar or bottle (it must be clear)

- A white or red candle to seal the jar.

- A gold, red, or silver color ribbon

The grains and seeds are totally up to you. Preferably, you should use what you already have at home. The rule is that they must be seven different varieties, for example: corn, lentils, rice, wheat (you can use pasta to represent wheat), beans or chickpeas, or fava beans.

Fill the jar with the grains and seeds one by one (so you can clearly see the seven levels). They should not be scrambled, but rather try to distinguish each little level through the jar.

Once you fill it, close it and seal it with red or white wax.

Decorate with ribbons, coins, or your favorite saint of devotion medal; it's totally up to you.

Año Viejo Doll Ritual

This is one of my favorite rituals for New Year's Eve, especially when we have had a really bad year, and we want to have a clean start for the new one. This ritual is as simple as making a doll representing an old man and burning it with a list of the things you would like to leave behind. This ritual is very common in Mexico; you can buy this type of doll from a lot of brujas or at the botanica. The doll can be burned on the first of January too, if you would like to focus on other rituals on the 31st of December.

I make my own dolls because I have the time and I think you get a better result that way. If you buy one in Mexico, be cautious, since these dolls contain gun powder (*pólvora*), and some others contain gasoline products.

To make your own, you are going to need different color fabrics, your own hair, foam to fill the doll, and twelve cloves.

It's very easy to create the doll. Just cut the fabric in the shape of the doll, paint a face, sew it together, and fill with your hair and the foam. We never throw out hair in the comb or the brush because it must be burned at the end of the year. Once the doll is filled, close it and we proceed to burn it with the list of the things we want to leave behind to start the next year fresh.

Open Roads for the New Year

This ritual is one of the easiest to do and a Mexican favorite. You can use a candle in the shape of a key or any old key that you have available. In this way you are going to open your roads magically for the year to come.

You will need:

- A key-shaped candle or an old key

- A plain candle in the appropriate color according to your desire (yellow for money, red for love, green for work, pink for friendship, and so on)

- Abre caminos oil

- Seven coins

- Your favorite herb to dress a candle

- Wooden matches

- A Mexican clay plate

On December 31, we will write our name on the candle. We will put it in the center of the clay plate and dress it with the abre caminos oil and your favorite herb. (If you cannot find abre caminos oil, you can use rosemary and olive oil.) It is extremely important to say the prayer with faith, visualizing your roads opening to reach what you want and need!

Distribute the seven coins in a circle around the candle-key. We will light the candle-key with wooden matches and recite the following prayer while concentrating:

In the name of the Father, the Son, and the Holy Spirit, shall
the doors open, shall my paths be cleared, shall the Divine Light
illuminate and Bless all my paths and lead me to achieve what

I'm planning for (here say the coming year) to fulfill my goals and dreams (here say your goals and dreams).

So be it.

After the candle is consumed, the coins will be placed in a pot outside near the door of the house or apartment.

Rituals for Travel

December holidays—besides festivities, food, and family gatherings—can be the perfect time to magically work on our goals, performing various rituals to bring good fortune, health, and abundance in the coming year. Among these rituals is the tradition of walking with luggage in the New Year. If you have been following my Instagram, you know I love to travel. I like go to other places, meet other people, and try other food. A lot of people might think that I have a lot of money to be able to travel at least five times per year, but the honest truth is that this ritual has helped me get invited places, get awesome deals, and I even won a trip to Los Cabos in a raffle back in 2018.

This ritual consists of going in and out of your house with your suitcase one time for every trip you have planned or that you would like to do in the next year. You can gather all the suitcases you have in your home and do this ritual as a family activity (this is only in case you want to take your children to those trips). Do not get embarrassed or shy as you are doing this. You will see a lot of people doing this in Mexico during the holiday season and their tipsy neighbors as well.

Los Calzones: The Underwear

We all have our own personal New Year's Eve traditions and practices for good luck. Some cultures' rituals date back hundreds of years. There's one tradition that might be strange in other places in the world. Perhaps not many people have ever heard about it: wearing red or yellow underwear on the night of New Year's Eve. Yes, it's believed to be a good luck charm if you wear red or yellow underwear the night of the big ball drop in Mexico.

There are a couple of "rules" one must follow to get the full New Year's luck associated with this tradition. First, most grandmothers' versions of this tradition state that the underwear must be a gift, which is perfect because a lot of people in Mexico use this as a Christmas gift idea with the intention that the gift will be used on New Year's Eve. Second, it must be a new pair of underwear that you wear for the first time on New Year's Eve. To be completely honest I have had to buy my own. I've even crafted my own bicolor panties for New Year's Eve.

The colors represent what we want to attract for the following year.

- Red for love matters and passion

- Yellow for money travel and trade

So, if you want an inexpensive gift full of magic, I recommend buying some *calzones* to give away on Christmas to your friends and family.

Twelve Grapes for New Year's Eve

Twelve grapes, twelve seconds, twelve wishes. This is the tradition of eating grapes at the stroke of midnight.

In Mexico everyone gets a bowl or skewer of twelve grapes just before midnight. I remember doing this as a child. It was super fun, but also a bit messy. On each stroke of the clock at midnight, you eat one grape. One for the first stroke, your second on the second stroke, etc. If you manage all twelve, you will have a lucky year. As for the number twelve, it is believed that the twelve grapes symbolize the months of the year.

As we all know, grapes can be a choking hazard, especially for young children. If in doubt, please cut your grapes in half lengthwise.

La Mazorca Dorada: Gold Corn

For overall prosperity, money, and protection in the coming year, you will need:

- A yellow *mazorca* (dry the ears and leave the corn husk on)

- Gold and silver acrylic paint

- Paint brushes

- Money drawing oil, Venus' Oil, or blessed olive oil

- A red bow, green bow, or any bow to hang behind your door

- Gold and/or silver glitter (totally up to your creativity)

- A copy or a drawing of the highest denomination bill of your country (you can use children's play money or Monopoly money)

On a Friday or a Sunday before New Year's Eve (I usually combine the two by doing it on Friday on the Sun's hour or Sunday on Venus's hour; you can easily find these correspondences using an app or by searching online), grab your already dry mazorca and mix a little bit of acrylic paint, and paint it, focusing on money, prosperity, and protection. Let it dry.

Add a little bit of clear glue and glitter and decorate the ribbon, the bill, and the husk, leaving a cord so you can hang it behind your door.

Once it is ready, you can hang it on New Year's Eve to maximize protection for your property as well. If you are not the crafty type, you can find mazorcas already painted in botanicas and hierberias during this time of year.

El Ruido para Espantar a los Malos Espiritus: To Ward Away Evil Spirits

In many parts of Mexico, it is customary to set off fireworks to celebrate the New Year. It is thought to be a way to ward away evil spirits and, with them, the bad luck of the coming year. It must be said that firing weapons, such as guns, to celebrate the new year is dangerous and against the law. This is possibly one of the most popular traditions and has claimed the lives of hundreds of children and adults and left behind an endless number of injured people because of these stray bullets.

When I immigrated to the United States, I left behind these traditions, which are even more common in the ranches, and I started focusing on new ones. But the first New Year's Eve my husband and I spent together, he handed me a pot and a metal spoon, and then he went outside. We ran around the house, banging on our pots and pans with our spatulas and metal spoons, making noises like crazy people. At the beginning, I did not get it, but once he explained, I remembered that we did the same thing at the same time to receive the new year, but in a much riskier way.

Soon I realized that the root of this custom was not Mexican or German, like my husband. It is actually Roman. The Spanish brought it to Mexico. So, the goal and the mechanics will remain the same: make a lot of noise. You can even buy noisemakers at the dollar store to give to the little kids in your family, your nieces and nephews. Next New Year's Eve, stay up late, watch the ball drop, eat your twelve grapes, and do not forget to make a lot of noise.

El Ritual de las Tres Monedas: The Three Coins Ritual

This prayer is prayed on the first Friday of the year. After praying, deposit three coins in the collection box of your local parish, chapel, or house of worship. If you don't feel comfortable attending church, these coins can instead be donated to any charity.

Receive, oh Lord, these three coins that I deposit here for the worship of your Divine Providence, let them be the proof of the three major powers of my soul: memory, intellect, and will, that are always protected under your blood, and at the same time I ask you to bless me at all times with a home in which to live, with clothing to cover myself, and my daily bread.

In the name of the Father, I deposit the first coin, in the name of the Son, the second coin, in the name of the Holy Spirit, the third. Your Divine Providence extends at every moment so that we never lack a house, clothing, and sustenance and our economic needs do not cause us torment.

Amen.

Saint Clair's Magical Rompope

Americans have eggnog, Puerto Ricans have *coquito*, Venezuelans have *ponche crema*, and Mexicans have *rompope*! This eggnog has minimal variations and can be adapted to your favorite drink or taste. It can be as universal as you want it to be, and you can totally tweak the recipe a little. Every area of Mexico, and maybe even every family, has its own recipe for rompope. My family's recipe just happened to be magical.

The story goes that, in the Convent of Santa Clara, in the city of Puebla, the Claretian nuns oversaw the kitchen management. They created many recipes, including this eggnog with a mixture of almonds and rum, giving the drink that unique taste that we know today.

Rompope contains approximately 15 percent alcohol, although you can adjust it if you want a lighter version. For this reason, you must be careful when consuming it in case you are sensitive to this type of drink. Do not offer it to a minor.

If you think about it, the egg is really a magical ally for a lot of Mexicans. After all, an egg is representative of a new life. It is a symbol of renewal and new starts. For that reason, rompope is the most magical drink for this time of the year. I especially love to drink it during New Year's Eve.

> 5 cups of whole milk
> 1 cup of brown sugar
> ¼ teaspoon baking soda
> 3 cinnamon sticks
> 3 whole cloves
> ⅛ teaspoon grated nutmeg
> 10 egg yolks
> 1 cup of rum (you can totally make it more "festive" by adding more)
> 2 teaspoons vanilla extract

In a pot over medium heat, combine milk, sugar, baking soda, cinnamon sticks, cloves, and nutmeg, and bring to a simmer. Turn off the heat and let the spices steep in the milk for twenty minutes. While the milk is steeping, set up a large bowl with a strainer over it near the stove. After the milk has steeped and cooled for twenty minutes, whisk the egg yolks in a bowl and stir into the milk, whisking constantly. Turn the heat back on to medium-low and cook the milk and egg mixture, stirring constantly until the mixture is thick enough to coat the back of a spoon.

Immediately strain the mixture to stop cooking and remove the cinnamon sticks, cloves, and any curds that may have started to form. Stir in the rum and vanilla extract.

Let it chill and store in glass bottles.

Tape a Saint Clare prayer card to the glass bottle. You can decorate with a Christmassy bow for the holidays.

Due to its ingredients, homemade eggnog may not last as long as other alcoholic beverages. A refrigerated eggnog can last for about three to four days. But if you want to extend its shelf life, I do recommend using pasteurized eggs.

Although there is a traditional recipe for rompope, it is a well-known fact that there is an unknown ingredient in the original formula, and that it was kept as a secret. My grandmother used to say that it was a toast in the form of a prayer, and that one of the Claretian nuns had commented to her that that was the secret. She made her own prayer that I translated to English and share with you today.

Prayer to Santa Clara

You who are at my table and your charity serve me of all kinds of opportunities, clarify doubts, clarify my vision, and clarify everything that is unclear.

Today I ask you to clarify this new year, to clear all illness, all misfortune, and all bad luck.

May that with hard work and care we achieve what we set out to do.

That like you, we will defend what we believe in, and we will continue working for it.

Show me things as they are but clarify my thoughts, my fears, and my life today and the year to come on this toast.

Salud!

Twelve Divine Providence Candles

Every year, on first day of January, thousands of Mexicans celebrate a beautiful tradition, which is accompanied by a very famous ritual. This ritual is somehow mystical and magical as well; It is a sign of faith and a magnificent way to start a new year. This is the ritual of blessing the candles of Divine Providence.

The ritual consists of going to the nearest church on the first day of the year to bless twelve candles, which will then be lit in prayer every first day of the month for the twelve months of the year. With this ritual, we will ensure that good health, employment, shelter, and blessings are never lacking in our homes. If for some reason you can't or don't want to go to church, you can give the candles a blessing yourself. The important thing is to have faith in the Lord's providence. It is recommended that you hold a family gathering on the first day of the month to light the candle and give thanks for everything received, as well as ask for what may be missing in our home.

January 1st

January 1 is the *cruda* day (the official hangover day). During New Year's Eve parties, most people in Mexico tend to consume excessive amounts of food and alcoholic beverages. The latter can cause the so-called hangover or, as this discomfort is colloquially known as la cruda.

The human body requires some effort to get rid of the toxins it received the night before, since alcohol is usually a toxic substance for the body after ingesting certain quantities. Thus, there are several methods, some more magical than others, to rid ourselves of toxins, and this one that I am going to mention does not fail.

Santa Bibiana Serum

This is a favorite in the grandmothers' repertoire. Club soda, sugar, salt, and the cleansing nature of lime is a practical combination that we Mexicans resort to with great faith.

Some know this recipe as Santa Bibiana's *suerito* and others call it "little angels." All you must do is mix club soda, lemon, sugar, and salt, and, while stirring, repeat the following prayer:

Santa Bibiana de los bebedores, quitales la cruda a estos cabrones.

Holy Bibiana of the drinkers, take the hangover off these bastards.

This recipe is usually prepared in a large pitcher, since it is not just one person who wakes up with a terrible hangover.

For the best results, serve breakfast. *Menudo, pozole,* or very spicy *chilaquiles* are recommended.

Borreguito de la Abundancia: Abundance's Lucky Sheep

Something quite traditional and my personal favorite ritual is to place a fabric sheep made of wool or other materials on top of the main door or on the inside doorknob as a way to attract abundance, considering that the sheep is an animal that will bring money to our home. (Don't forget that Mexicans colloquially refer to money as *lana,* meaning wool.) Leave the lucky sheep up for the holidays and save it to re-use next year.

Predict the Weather with las Cabañuelas

It is worth mentioning that *cabañuelas* (a method of predicting the weather) have no scientific basis, but it is a strong and popular belief that has been transmitted from generation to generation. The method is as follows: the first twelve days of January represent a month in ascending order, so (January 1 represents January, January 2 is February, January 3 is March, and so on. For example, if January 1 is sunny, January is expected to be dry and hot, while if January 4 is rainy, April is expected to be wet and cold. If January 6 shows clear skies and heat, it is associated with a clear and hot June.

Epiphany Tradition

This beautiful tradition is very old in Mexico and other countries. It consists of marking your door with chalk in this way:

20 + C + M + B + 23

- The numbers on either end of the equation are from the year 2023.

- The letters are the initials of the Latin prhase *Christus Mansionem Benedicat* which means (Christ bless this house). They also represent the initials of the Magi in Latin, *Caspar, Melchior et Baltassar* (Gaspar, Melchor, and Baltazar).

- The signs (+) represent the Cross.

This is done so that Christ may bless your home and those who live there throughout the year. Traditionally the blessing is done by a priest or the father of the family, but this is folk Catholicism at its core, so you can do it yourself. After marking the door (or above on the door frame) offer a short prayer. If you do not have your own prayer, you can easily find one online.

Los Reyes Magos

Every January 6, Mexico celebrates the tradition of the Magi, where the story goes that the Three Wise Men came from the Far East, guided by a bright star. Tradition dictates that children write a letter to the Three Wise Men asking them for the gifts they would like to receive. On the eve of the festival (January 5th), shoes are filled with a little straw that is used to feed the animals that accompany the Three Wise Men. The straw disappears on January 6, and the children run to look for their shoes to find their gifts. Modern ways to write to the Three Wise Men include helium ballons and regular mail.

This ritual is inspired by what we did when we were children in Mexico. You will need:

- Gold (you can use pyrite or an old broken chain) to represent a mundane wish, like material blessings, money, properties, income

- Incense (preferably in resin, but you can also use incense sticks or cones) to represent a spiritual wish, like protection, wisdom, good luck

- *Mirra*/myrrh (I prefer resin, but if you don't have it, you can use a myrrh incense stick) to represent a mortal wish (something in your life that you would like to die, such as a habit, a situation, a relationship, etc.)

- A representation of a star (I'm going to use my *loteria* card)

- A white candle (the size does not matter.)

On the night of the fifth, you will put these ingredients, in the order that you have gathered them, in front of a Three King's statue and the representation of the star. If you do not have the Three Kings statue, do it in the old-fashioned Mexican way and use your shoes. You will focus on your three wishes one by one and light the candle, visualizing them.

At the end you will give thanks, as if you had already received these gifts. You will see how these three wishes will soon manifest into your life.

Write a Letter to Los Reyes Magos

Writing a letter to the Three Wise Men is a very deep-rooted Mexican tradition. Although the objective is the same, letters to the Three Wise Men vary depending on the child who writes them. In general, you can find letters with drawings, letters in envelopes, or cards. This tradition is so magical that it shouldn't be lost when we reach adulthood.

To make a wish, you need only a sheet of paper, a pen, and a helium balloon. My letter has always been the same since I arrived in the US.

Queridos reyes magos:

My wish for this day is the wish of the children who had to immigrate to this country, due to situations totally independent to them or even their own parents. In my "Three Kings Day" letter I ask a dignified life, a path to citizenship for them and their parents, and social guarantees, a right that should not be denied to anyone regardless of their immigration status, because a child who grows up without social security and dreams, in this immigration limbo, will accept without protest labor slavery, alms from wages, and oppression by the authorities due to fear. That is why we are obliged to guarantee our kids, by all the necessary means, today and always, their right to happiness, having the same opportunities for health, permanence, and inclusion as any child who has been born on this side of the border.

My wish on Three Kings Day is that all those children have a path to their citizenship, a fair one.

Just as my children had dreamed about many days of kings for many years.

Once you write the letter, fold it and tie it to the balloon, then release the balloon with a lot of faith.

BIBLIOGRAPHY

Arendzen, J. P., Flynn, Thomas E., et. al.195, *Diccionario enciclopédico de la Fe Católica*, Editorial Jus. México.

————. *Brujería* mexicana, Use su poder para lograr lo que desea. Editoriales mexicanos unidos 2003. México.

Canedo Zamora, Gerardo. *Los poderes de la magia. Magia blanca y magia negra.* Editoriales mexicanos unidos 2006. México.

Carrión, Jorge. *Mito y magia del mexicano.* Editorial Nuestro Tiempo, 1952. México.

de la Luz Bernal, María S. *Mitos y magos mexicanos*, 2da edición Editorial posada. January 1, 1982. México.

El Grande, Alberto. *El libro supremo de todas las magias.* la magia blanca secreta y adivinatoria arte nueva de hechar las cartas y la baraja española 1977. México.

González Gómez, José Antonio. "Juan Minero: una devoción popular novo-hispana." *academia.edu*

González Mello, Renato "Palafox: donde están los peritos, camotes no satis-facen" en El Alcaraván: Boletín trimestral del Instituto de Artes Gráficas de Oaxaca, Vol. II, N° 7, Oct-Nov-Dic de 1991, IAGO. México.

Lara, Karen. *Formulario moderno de hechicería.* Edamex 1988. México.

————. *Los grandes secretos de la magia blanca.* Producciones Karen Lara. Primera impresión 1997. México.

Lara, Karen. *Recetas mágicas para la abundancia.* KL Editor 2005. México.

Lopez Ridaura, Cecilia. "Que sosiego no encuentre": impresos damnificatorios. Boletín de Literatura Oral, vol. extraordinario 2. 2019. *academia.edu*

Masera, Mariana. *Literatura y culturas populares de la nueva España.* Azul Editorial, 2004. México.

Nacional Autónoma de México, Instituto de Investigaciones Antropológicas, Plaza y Valdés, 1996, 303 p. México.

Polanco, Horacio. *Recetas mágicas para resolver sus problemas.* Grupo editorial Tomo, S.A de C.V. 1era edición, Enero 1999. México.

Quezada, Noemi. *El curandero colonial representante de una mezcla de culturas,* en Historia general de la medicina en México. Medicina novohispana siglo xvi, México, Academia Nacional de Medicina, Universidad Nacional Autónoma de México, Facultad de Medicina, 1990, p. 313-327. México.

———. *Enfermedad y maleficio.* El curandero en el México colonial, México, Universidad Nacional Autónoma de México, Instituto de Investigaciones Antropológicas, 1989. México.

———. *Amor y magia amorosa entre los aztecas,* México, Universidad Nacional Autónoma de México, Instituto de Investigaciones Antropológicas, 1996. México.

———. *Sexualidad, amor y erotismo: México prehispánico y México colonial,* México, Universidad. México.

Sepúlveda y Herrera, Maria Teresa. *Magia, brujería y supersticiones en México, Colección Raíces mexicanas.* Editorial Everest Mexicana Enero 1983, México.

Tamara. *Brujeria, hechizos conjuros y encantamientos.* Grupo editorial Tomo, S.A de C.V. 2da edición, Marzo 1999, México.

———. *Magia blanca: Pequeño recetario de hechizos y conjuros.* Grupo editorial Tomo, S.A de C.V. 1era edición, 2000, México.

———. *Gran manual de magia casera.* Grupo editorial Tomo, S.A de C.V. 1era edición, Octubre 2005, México.

issuu.com/vanguardiamedia

ABOUT THE AUTHOR

Laura Davila is a fifth-generation Mexican witch, a long-time practitioner of Mexican *ensalmeria, hechicería, brujeria,* and folk Catholicism. Born and raised in Mexico, Laura has lived in the United States since 2010. Laura identifies as a *bruja de rancho*—a "ranch witch"—a term with great resonance in Mexico, indicating knowledge of botanicals and the natural world. The author of *Mexican Sorcery,* Laura is also a tarot card reader and a flower essence practitioner. Follow her on Instagram @daphne_la_hechicera

TO OUR READERS

Weiser Books, an imprint of Red Wheel/Weiser, publishes books across the entire spectrum of occult, esoteric, speculative, and New Age subjects. Our mission is to publish quality books that will make a difference in people's lives without advocating any one particular path or field of study. We value the integrity, originality, and depth of knowledge of our authors.

Our readers are our most important resource, and we appreciate your input, suggestions, and ideas about what you would like to see published.

Visit our website at *www.redwheelweiser.com*, where you can learn about our upcoming books and free downloads, and also find links to sign up for our newsletter and exclusive offers.

You can also contact us at *info@rwwbooks.com* or at

Red Wheel/Weiser, LLC
65 Parker Street, Suite 7
Newburyport, MA 01950